"Randy helped us realize that the answers lie within yourself. As a PGA Tour Caddy I learned how to use Randy's concepts, and help my player (my brother Kevin Na) to 'get out of his own way.' I was amazed to witness that when Kevin used Randy's mind power techniques, it resulted in such a huge improvement, and so quickly. Now I can help him stay focused and positive for the entire four rounds. Randy's book, *Your Inner Swing* will help move you to the next level... it did for us!"

Austin Na, Professional PGA Tour Caddy to Kevin Na

"Randy has been able to take the life information I give her and develop a session that fits my needs. We have done this on several occasions as issues arose, and each time I have been able to see positive results. I encourage golfers to work with Randy to achieve the same kind of positive results I have."

Bobby Heins, Two-time Metropolitan PGA player of the year
PGA Head Professional
Old Oaks CC, Purchase, NY (25 Years +)

"For years I've sought numerous teachers to fix my 'chip yips.' After one Mind Power session with Randy, she not only fixed the problem, but gave me the tools that helped me get out of my own way to play better under pressure. I highly recommend *Your Inner Swing*."

Freddie Dolan, (4 Hcp), President, StretchMate, Inc.
PGA Tour Players Flexibility Coach

"Randy helped us make the Saturday Series Private Outing for the PGA Tour and Golf Channel a huge success. It takes somebody who is very confident of their abilities to work comfortably in the loose structure we prefer at our events. The clinic was very well received, both by the guests and the Tour professionals. I know I will be telling people about the things I learned listening to Randy and Ted Purdy interact. That was top-notch stuff!"

John Goutell, Chief Operating Officer
Saturday Series Pro-Am a PGA Tour official event

"*Your Inner Swing* will help free your mind to play the game you were meant to play."

Shad Muth, Professional Golfer, Gateway Tour
Mr. "59" Hastings, MN

Your Inner Swing

7 Lessons in Golf ... and Life!

RANDY FRIEDMAN

Copyright © 2008 by Randy Friedman

yourinnerswing.com

All rights reserved. No part of this publication may be reproduced, stored in a retrieval system, or transmitted, in any form or by any means, electronic, mechanical, photocopying, recording, or otherwise, without the prior written permission of the publisher.
Printed in the United States of America.

Cataloging-in-Publication Data for this book is available from the Library of Congress.

Friedman, Randy
Parisi, Anthony J. - Illustrator
Toropov, Brandon - Editor
ISBN -13:978-O-9817447-1-1
ISBN-13: 978-O-9817447-2-8

10 9 8 7 6 5 4 3 2

DEDICATION

This book is dedicated to the the two people who brought me into this world, my Mom and Dad. I am the sum of your parts — good, bad, indifferent — and a whole lot greater because of you both.

You taught me that the grass is not always greener on the other side, and to be aware that change is good.

You taught me that doors are going to close, and when they do, to be ready for the new ones that will open.

You allowed me to be different from everyone else, to find my own path, to beat my own drum and to discover new journeys.

You never stopped me from wandering, you just put bells on my feet so you could find me when I did.

You punished me when I did wrong, and always praised me when I did right.

Thank you, thank you, thank you, Mom and Dad! May the life foundation you shared with me become a beacon of life that I can share with others.

CONTENTS

Acknowledgments   ix

Introduction   1
    Why this book is for you.

1 Beliefs   11
    What is your pre-shot routine ... for everything you do? Look closely at what you believe about yourself, your golf, and your world.

2 Awareness   27
    Are you focusing on what's holding you back ... or on what could be moving you forward? Notice what you're telling yourself and what your emotional responses are.

3 Gratitude   45
    Do you love playing golf yet? Give sincere thanks for all you have received in your life.

4 Goals   61
    Focus only on what you want. By the way, what DO you want on the golf course today?

5 Attitude   87
    Assess your attitude, and the self it reveals. Is that really who you want to be?

6 Garden   89
    What are you growing? Where are you going? If you want to know ... open the Garden that exists within you.

7 Energy   101
    Tap into the life force! How are you responding to the negative energy of others? What kind of energy are you drawing into your golf – and your life.

Epilogue   117
    Are you ready to push the button? Faith is all you need to build the Inner Swing that is right for you.

Appendix   121
    Simple activities that will help you to connect your Golf Mind Power.

ACKNOWLEDGMENTS

… to Rose who supported me from day one with the very best "you can do anything you set your mind to" attitude! I am so grateful for the love and support you've always given me. Thank you, for being my sunrise and sunset, my food, my water, and my internal breath!

… to mom and dad for more than I can possibly list here.

… to my sisters Lori and Shelley, for always reminding me that because I was the baby I could always get anything and everything I wanted! I know now that if you just hear it long enough that is what you believe! Thank you for always being there for me. Michael and Vic, thanks for keeping my sisters smiling!

… to my very special Elyse Mara (Elyse-tress), Morgan Bailey (Morga-moo) and Jacob Zachary (Jake-ster). Watching you three grow up from birth has been one of my greatest joys. You three continue to bring sunshine into my Garden like nothing else ever could.

… to Tony and Donna. I cherish our relationship and thank you for your love and support.

… to Heshie and Glo - you're both great! Glo I've never met a stronger Survivor.

… to Mom and Mom Glo - my Survivors, my inspiration for life. To all breast cancer survivors around the world, thank you for your courage to press on and for sharing your story with us. In our lifetime, we will see a cure.

… to Brandon Toropov, my editor and literary genius! I could not have produced the book that this has become without you. You pushed me in all the right directions and brought *Your Inner Swing* to bright life! I thank you for finding me.

… to Anthony Parisi, the finest illustrator a girl from Kindergarten class could find. My memories of you at Davis Elementary are of you drawing Star Trek illustrations… and it seems your early developmental skills paid off! You really made *Your Inner Swing* jump off the shelf! I thank you for your wonderful illustrations.

… to Mike Smith for opening my eyes to the best game in the world, and showing me the initial path to my inner self. I never knew about motivational speakers until you shared your insight with me. Thank you for giving me a chance to make a difference.

… to John Redd, my first golf coach, who taught me that discipline comes from an inner desire to know what you want and find out how to get it. Thank you for my life lesson ... to rake a bunker smooth, is to read every green!

… to Phyllis and Larry Uchin, Richard and Susan Katcher, Jack and Marsha Petcove, Mary and Paul Humenansky, Marsha Showstead, Rob Ohno, Eve, Scott, Alexandra, Giuliana and Scotti Trivella, Brian Crowell, Kristi Gomen, Austin Na, Kevin Na, Bobby Heins, Freddie Dolan, John Goutell, Shad Muth, Dr. Paula Fellingham, Nancy Henderson, Patti Benson, Helen West, Lowell C. Douglas, Lynn Blake, Paul Fink, Alana Friedlander, Marlene Mulder, Randall Churchill, Tom Preece, Tom Campbell, Al Chance, Jeff Kerman, A.J. Ali, Paul de Barros, Mary Lynn Pearlman, Gene Borek and Ellen Boyle for all their help, support, inspiration, and encouragement along the way.

INTRODUCTION

Read This First

> *Teachers can open the door, but you must enter by yourself.*
>
> Chinese proverb

"...Inhale deeply through your nose and fill up your lungs ... hold it .... now take another sip in ... and another ..."

Is she kidding, I thought? I don't have another sip!

But I did...somehow; I got more air into my lungs. I stayed with it ... and I did manage to take in another sip of air!

"Your goal is to fill up that five-quart capacity in your lungs," the yoga teacher continued. *"Believe in yourself. You can do it. Now slowly ... slowly ... exhale through your nose, feeling that the life energy within*

your muscles has been retained. It's that life energy that allows us to go beyond our limitations, the restrictions we've all put on ourselves."

That's when it hit me about the golfer's belief system. The golfer's real handicap is held within: the inner, mental swing, rather than the outer, physical swing.

Handicaps have not come down over the years. Why not? Because of the internal handicaps we've put on ourselves. *Your inner swing* has been blocking your outer swing, which should be, and could be, perfect.

Fortunately, *your inner swing* is about to change.

BEYOND LIMITATIONS

This book is offered with unconditional love as a tool for helping you overcome perceived limitations in your golf game ... even if you've tried to overcome physical limitations before and been unable to do so. This book is meant to change forever the quality of golf in your life ... and the quality of life in your golf.

A lot of that change has to do with your perception of yourself ... and the way you breathe through your life. Think for just a moment about the importance of breath. How long can you go without food? Weeks. How long can you go without water? Days. How long can you go without air? Minutes. *Breathing matters!*

HOW DO YOU DEFINE LIFE?

I define "life" as the existence that passes between our first breath in and our last breath out. It is the *quality* of the existence between those breaths that allows us to live life fully ... or absently. This idea of living fully, presently, ties into golf in a way that is actually fairly simple, yet at the same time, quite profound.

Developing *your inner swing* is about going inside, and evaluating your internal systems — like your breathing, for instance. Whenever we struggle, are fearful, or try too hard to make something happen, our breathing becomes labored and shallow. This keeps us tense, frightened,, and more likely to get in our own way. In short, poor breathing makes it impossible for us to perform at our highest level. Breathing may not seem to have anything to do with your golf game ... but in fact, it does, because it affects what's going on inside of you.

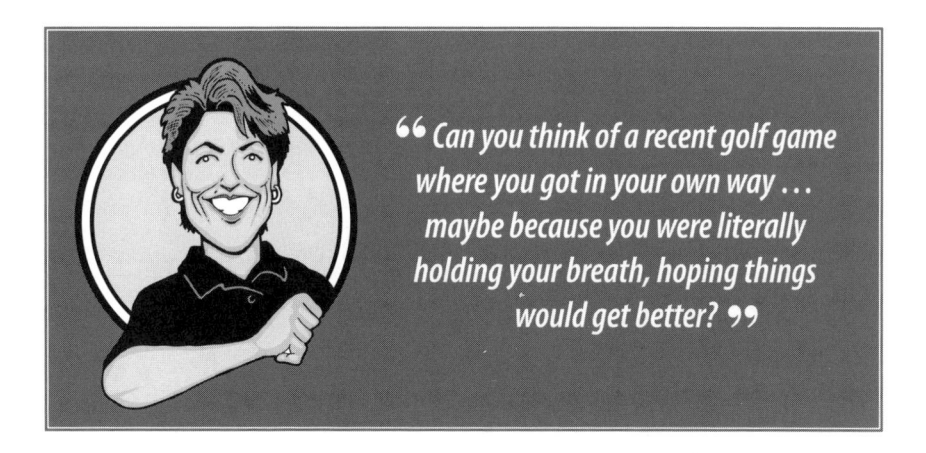

> **"** *Can you think of a recent golf game where you got in your own way ... maybe because you were literally holding your breath, hoping things would get better?* **"**

By the way, are you breathing deeply right now? If you've been struggling with your golf game – or your larger life — at any point, the odds are good that you've been holding your breath or simply not breathing deeply enough when you felt stressed. Take a deep breath right now. Notice how it makes you feel.

Do you want to increase your mental clarity, concentrate with ease, develop your creative imagination, and lower your golf score? Then keep reading ... and keep breathing.

What are you looking for? Are you looking for a few simple, instructional pictures? Are you looking for step-by-step diagrams that will help you "improve your swing"? Are you looking for a couple of quick ideas on "how to do it"?

Maybe you've already leafed through the main section of this book, hoping to find a quick tip or two — something specific that you could physically use on the golf course tomorrow, or practice for that company outing that's coming up next week. Maybe you're looking for something that would instantly help you become a better golfer right now. You didn't find any. That's because there isn't anything like that here.

Before you consider taking a pass on the rest of this book, or "skimming" it for the "key points," consider this:

- **You picked up this book for a reason.**
- **There are no accidents in this life**
- **If you want help that will "stick"...read on.**

Now that you're reading this ... what if I told you that improving your golf swing, and indeed your entire game, is a mental process first and foremost?

What if I told you that nothing you could paste on from the outside – no picture, no list of tips, no trick, no diagram showing you how to hold the club — could change the level of performance you can actually expect to achieve *and sustain* on the golf course?

What if I could give you something even better than the graphics and how-to tips you thought you were looking for when you picked up this book?

What if I could pass along, within these pages, something that has lowered the scores of thousands of golfers I've coached, and has made them happier and more complete people as well?

Keep going ...

MEET JOHN

John was a successful, career-driven hedge fund broker. He'd figured out how to "pull the trigger" professionally and make a lot of money, but he had no idea what to do on the golf course. He took lesson after lesson, and he read all the books on the "perfect golf swing" that he could find. Yet he was not improving.

John was focused on the "how" of his swing – or, to be more accurate, on the "how not to" of the game of golf. He wanted to stop slicing his tee shots, quit chunking his wedges, and put an end to three-putting.

The harder he tried not to do these things, the more he did them and the higher his score climbed.

When he came to me he was at his wit's end and ready to quit the game. He wanted a quick diagnosis and a quick fix. He didn't want to put a lot of time into his game; he simply wanted me to show him what he was doing wrong.

Before our first lesson began, I watched John being rude and short-tempered to his caddy. As he strode toward the driving range I noticed that John stopped to take a cell phone call from his wife; I couldn't help hearing how curt and hostile he was to her.

What happened next was amazing —- and a little disturbing. John ended the call with his wife. Once he was face-to-face with me, the golf pro, his whole attitude changed. Now he was pleasant, engaged, patient, and smiling broadly in anticipation of getting the answer to his question: "What am I doing wrong?" The answer I gave him wasn't what he expected.

Two weeks later, after just a couple of sessions, John was asking himself some different questions – and getting a different outcome. Not just on the course, where he easily improved his game, but more importantly, in his conversations with his wife, and interactions with his caddy! John had improved not just his game, *but his entire life.*

What happened?

How did the answers to "golf questions" become, at the same time, the answers to questions about the type of person John wanted to be? And ... **how did both sets of answers emerge within just a few weeks, after only two hours of focused coaching time?**

THREE SURPRISES

Here are three things that surprise the people I coach.

Surprise Number One: *Beliefs that improve your golf game will also improve your larger life.* It's a mistake to think of your beliefs and capabilities as operating separately, in two different worlds. You are who you are, both on the golf course and on "life's course."

Surprise Number Two: *You choose all the thoughts that guide you through golf AND through life.* We can always find a way to move past what I call "adult brain malfunction." That's the misguided thinking that's all about what we don't want; that's the habit of focusing on our tools, rather than on ourselves and our surroundings. In our golf, and in the larger game of life, we may come to believe that we are engaged in a ball game.

Actually, it's not a ball game. It's a target game. Kids get this instantly; adults sometimes have a little harder time with it. *Your job is the target, not the ball.* If you choose target thoughts, as opposed to ball thoughts, you'll be happier with the outcomes you get.

As things stand now, your approach may be like John's when I first started working with him. He was having difficulties with the club, difficulties with the course, difficulties with his wife, difficulties with

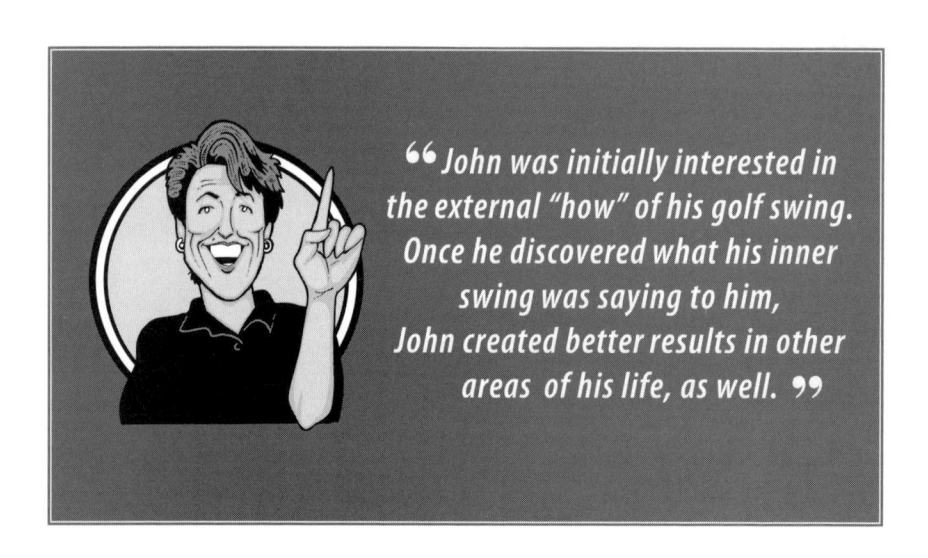

> **“** *John was initially interested in the external "how" of his golf swing. Once he discovered what his inner swing was saying to him, John created better results in other areas of his life, as well.* **”**

the time of day, difficulties with his own "bad habits." *John's focus was on everything negative; on everything that was "wrong" with his life.* He was suffering from "adult brain malfunction!" My job was to help him make the transition between "adult brain" and "childlike brain." And the choice really was John's to make — all the time.

Surprise Number Three: *Your transition from "adult brain" to "childlike brain" will be easy, not hard to make.* This is often the biggest surprise of all. Part of you already knows how to focus on the target. Part of you knows that the process of targeting something starts inside, not outside yourself. This ability to focus on yourself and your own feelings is basic human knowledge. It's already part of who you are, and it's one of your most important gifts, even if you may have stopped using it for a while. Once we learn to get out of our own way long enough and use the right mental approach, we can effortlessly hit the target we're intending to hit, without difficulty.

This will be easy. The ball will take care of itself. Honest.

WHAT JOHN REALLY LEARNED

The goal is to simply be open to the situation and get out of our own way. What stands in the way of that? Something I call Baggage.

There's nothing inherently wrong with having Baggage. In fact, we all have it. Baggage is basically your life story. It is what it is – the question is whether your Baggage is helping you move forward or holding you back.

Once you figure out exactly what your Baggage really is, and how it has been helping or hurting you, you can improve your inner and your outer game. Whenever you're ready, I can help you do it.

Here is what John really learned, and what I help all of my clients to learn: When you go within, you won't go without! Are you ready to start learning that *now?*

Then turn the page.

BELIEFS

AWARENESS

GRATITUDE

GOALS

ATTITUDE

GARDEN

ENERGY

> *" Your Baggage is what shapes your internal and external worlds. Everything about your golf game is connected to your adult Baggage. You'll be learning a lot about Baggage here... "*

Understand a few things about Baggage. It's nothing more or less than our "life story." Baggage is all the "stuff" we all hold in our minds. It's the "stuff" you've been carrying around for a long time, which you may or may not be aware of, that needs to be addressed if you really want to move forward in your golf game. Baggage is neither negative or positive. It's just there to be dealt with in one of two ways.

In any given area, your Baggage is either dynamic or static. When your Baggage is dynamic, you are full of energy, enthusiasm and have a sense of purpose on the golf course. You have the ability to get things moving, hit the shot, and get things done.

When you are in a static place with your Baggage, you are not moving or changing. You are for the most part fixed in a single position, encountering the same problems on the golf course over and over again.

When you spend more time in a dynamic space than in a static space, people notice and want to be around you. Golf becomes effortless and fun. This book is not about "getting rid of your Baggage" – instead, it's about making your Baggage work for you in a dynamic way.

Does this sound familiar?

ONE

BELIEFS

> *Believe in yourself! Have faith in your abilities! Without a humble but reasonable confidence in your own powers you cannot be successful or happy.*
>
> Norman Vincent Peale

"I thought this was a book about golf!"

Why bother with questions about what you believe, what you are aware of, whether you are grateful for what is happening in your life? Why take the time to discuss your goals? Why should you listen to someone who asks you about your garden, your attitude, and your energy? What does any of this have to do with golf?

Let me answer that question by posing another: What do MOST golfers spend their time on ... and what kinds of results do MOST golfers produce as a result?

Most of the golfers I meet focus on externals. And as a result, they never learn what they really need to learn in order to master their own game. They never learn what goes into a perfect inner swing, which is what makes the great external swing possible. Every visible "great swing" proceeds from a repeatable internal mental process. And that internal process is always guided by your beliefs.

If what you've been working on so far has been limited to things like how you stand, how you hold the club, and what your follow-through should look like ... you haven't been doing the mental work necessary to take your game to the next level.

Have you ever wondered how the golf professionals you see on TV do what they do? Have you ever watched them doing what they do, then gone out on the golf course to "try out" what you thought you saw?

HAVE YOU EVER EXPERIENCED THAT NOT WORKING?

Yes — the pros really do know something you don't know. They know something about their inner game. They know how to step into their "zone" of playing golf without thinking about technique.

THE PRE-SHOT ROUTINE

You may believe that the pros spend most of their time trying to improve the same things you are trying to improve: the externals. Here's where I want you to test that belief. The next time you watch a professional golf tournament on TV, pay special attention to the ten to twenty seconds before the golfer hits the ball. What you will find is that professionals invariably engage in a repeatable pre-shot routine that is timed with precision.

It is this consistent physical and mental ritual that prepares the golfer to see the shot in his or her "inner mind" before they actually hit the ball.

Think about your game. Do you do that?

Do you have some sort of pre-shot routine that settles your nerves and relaxes your mind before you step up to hit the shot?

Every professional golfer engages in this mental ritual of preparation, the pre-shot routine. Very few amateurs do.

> **" *Those few seconds of preparation that come before the club hits the ball constitute a swing that only the golfer sees - an INNER SWING.* "**

Only when professionals have mastered the inner swing can they make the best possible external swing.

What you are going to learn here is exactly what allows the top golf professionals to do what they do, each and every time they play the game.

Notice that you have just changed your beliefs about how important the inner swing is, and how the pre-shot routine can actually help you every time.

When you started reading this chapter, it's possible that you were more focused on the external pre-shot routine, and that you didn't consider how important a mental role the pre-shot routine actually plays.

Your inner swing **is nothing more or less than the process of preparing mentally, for the shot to come.**

Inner dialogue is the act of bringing your conscious and subconscious minds into agreement about exactly what is going to happen next, and how it is going to happen. It's the choice to cross what professional golfers call the "decision line." It's where you commit to making – rather than attempting to make – the best shot.

> *Try not. Do ... or do not. There is no try.*
>
> Yoda, from *The Empire Strikes Back*

If you're not examining your own internal dialogue before you swing at the ball, you have not yet mastered *your inner swing*.

BECOMING A MASTER MIND

You must have clear beliefs to produce the thoughts that help you. If you're not clear on what your current beliefs are or should be, this book is for you.

This book is all about taking conscious control of the mental aspect of your game, which is what makes mastery in the rest of your game possible. Developing dynamic beliefs – beliefs that support your growth — is one of the keys to learning to get out of your own way.

If you're like most of the people I coach, you will find that this focus on belief and internal dialogue will connect to many areas of your life other than golf. But make no mistake: I wrote this book about golf. Because golf is – or at least should be – fun!

If, as you swing the club, you're thinking about

- **how to take the club back**
- **pausing at the top**
- **and how you're going to finish the swing ...**

Then it is your inner swing, not your outer swing, that still needs work!

This is important — read it! If, as you swing the club, you're worried about what happened last time you were on this hole, and if you are picturing that happening again and telling yourself, "Don't do that," *your inner swing* still needs work.

> **"** *If, as you swing the club, you're focused on what you don't want to do ... your inner swing still needs work.* **"**

Granted, there's a place for mastering the physical aspects of the golf swing. As you may be aware, there is no shortage of instruction on the swing, but there's a vast gap when it comes to learning how to master the mental process of the inner swing.

Most of the tools golf instructors use to help students are connected exclusively to the physical portion of the game. The best work, however, takes place when the mental and physical work proceeds side by side. I'm going to assume that you already have some basic advice on the physical fundamentals. What follows is all about the beliefs that drive the mental game you bring to the golf course.

No external advice from me or anyone else on "how to swing" will help you unless your belief system supports you. You won't improve your game if you believe that it's improbable or impossible for you to do so. Your body will always respond to your thoughts because it does not judge your thoughts, it simply believes you either way and responds accordingly. If you really want to change what your body is doing, change your beliefs.

> *Whether you think you can or think you can't,
> either way you're right.*
>
> — Henry Ford

CHRIS'S STORY

I've worked with thousands of students over the years, and in all that time, only one person stands out in my mind as someone who was not open to receiving my help. Her name was Chris.

The first time I met Chris, she scheduled a half-hour lesson with me on the range. Within the first three minutes of the lesson I realized that her true problem was not a physical issue, but was actually mental. Chris was a textbook example of someone who had been "over-instructed" by taking too many lessons from too many different people looking for "the" answer. Her conscious mind was overflowing with countless negative beliefs about her swing. She had received so much instruction, and memorized so many different approaches, that she no longer had a clear picture of what she actually wanted to do. She spent most of the session telling me what was wrong! After she hit a shot, she would instantly look at me and say, "I came over the top that time, right?" Or she would say: "I was too flat that time, huh?"

She was so focused on what she was doing wrong that whatever positive suggestion I had for her, she instantly negated. In fact, Chris was constantly searching for evidence that she was doing something wrong. Her belief system told her that if she looked hard enough, she could find a mistake in her golf game… and every time she looked, that's exactly what she found!

Chris did most of the talking during our session. At the end of the half hour, I felt completely drained and knew I just could not help her.

I really felt I had failed her. I told her I thought the best thing for her to do would be just to go play golf … and not worry about her swing being perfect. I told her that she would do much better if she found a way to enjoy being out on the course.

There was no way that I could help Chris improve her inner game, because she was so fixated on the "mistakes" in the outer game. Her inner thoughts kept telling her to find something wrong with her swing… so she kept getting more of what she knew was wrong with her swing! Because she was so fixated on identifying the "mistakes" in her technique, it was impossible for her to relax and find her own game.

Look again at what Chris's real obstacle was:

She believed there was "something wrong with her golf swing." So that's exactly what she kept finding evidence for! That was the belief that was driving Chris … and it was the main thing that was keeping her from getting out of her own way!

I've learned a lot since then as a teacher and mind coach. If I had Chris as a student now, I would have applied a simple Mind Power technique with her, the kind of inner mind relaxation technique that I'm going to be sharing with you later in the book. This is a simple strategy for "entering the flow" that settles down the conscious, critical mind and lets you non-critically accept and focus on what you really want to believe about yourself.

I'd like to think that Chris will someday read this book. When she does, I know I will have finally been able to help her get out of her own way.

That's all I ever do with any of my students, by the way: Help them get out of their own way … so they can perform at the level they choose, both inside and out. The first and probably most essential step to getting out of your own way is understanding your own self-limiting beliefs.

Your beliefs drive everything, including your golf game. Once you know what your current beliefs really are, once you realize beliefs about yourself are something you can actually choose …the sky is the limit!

> **IN THE ZONE**
>
> ❝ *Golfers learn best when they actually lose themselves in the enjoyable process of relaxing and "finding their own game". We call this being "in the flow" or "in the zone." Most children are often in the zone.* ❞

WHY GOLF IS 90% MENTAL

Golf is a mental game. You've heard that so often that it may have become a cliché for you. Do you "know" intellectually, that golf is "90% mental?" If so, I want to ask you:

> *What have you done with that knowledge?*
> *Have you changed the way you think?*
> *Have you changed what you believe?*
> *Have you applied a new belief to some aspect of your game?*

Like many clichés, the one about golf being primarily a mental game is popular for the simple reason that it is fundamentally true.

Golf, unlike some other sports, gives you plenty of time to think before you hit the shot. Ironically though, most people either don't use that time well, or use it to "over-think" what they're about to do, by painting pictures in their minds of the shot going wrong. The less time you take to "consciously" think over what could go wrong with a given shot, the more you harness your inner mind's subconscious power to accomplish the immediate goal of hitting the target.

> *A belief is not merely an idea the mind possesses;*
> *It's an idea that possesses the mind.*
>
> Robert Oxton Bolt, English playwright

BELIEFS CONTROL PHYSICAL DEMANDS

Jack, a 10-handicap golfer, came to me because, in his words, he "wasn't scoring like he used to." Jack physically was very good at the game, but he realized that something other than his physical skills were keeping him from getting to where he wanted to be. When I asked him why he wanted to work with me, he said, "I've practiced and worked on my swing long enough to realize that there must be something more to this game … something that I'm unaware of." And he was right. There is.

Typically, people I work with say things to me like, "My goal is to break 100, but I'm a bad putter; I want you to fix my lousy putting."

What are you communicating to yourself with a statement like that?

"Watch, I'm a lousy putter."

What are you telling yourself when you're out on the golf course?

"Remember to be a lousy putter out here!"

Guess what?

It's your belief that you're "a lousy putter" that is actually causing the problem!

YOU CREATED THAT BELIEF, probably because you hit some bad putts along the way. Those bad putts provided "evidence" that you were a lousy putter. This experience reinforced your belief that you were a lousy putter. Before you hit your next putt you had a new internal mantra that said:

"Hey, you're a bad putter. Make sure you miss this."

That's the essence of what you're saying, even though you may think you're saying or thinking something else.

The belief that you are a "bad putter" is what is energizing the experience and delivering the outcome of bad putts.

It's almost as though you were ordering "bad putting" like room service at a hotel. The act of focusing on "bad putting" or "I don't putt well" is you putting in the call to the front desk. "Give me more bad putting, please! I want to miss this putt and I want to miss more putts."

- What do you believe about yourself?
- What do you keep reinforcing about yourself?
- What are you ordering from your personal room service?

When you repeat the mantra, "I hope I don't miss it," what you're really saying is, "Miss it." The words "I hope I don't" vanish because our imagination sees only the pictures in the message we send. Since there is no possible image for the word "don't," our imagination connects to the first image it encounters … which is the image of us missing the ball!

Read it again! It's that important!

Since there is no possible image for the word "don't," our imagination connects to the first image it encounters … which is the image of us missing the ball!

> **❝ The human IMAGINATION is a creative force that works by means of the IMAGES we feed it.**
> **It can process only the PICTURES in the messages we send it … and the bigger and brighter the PICTURE is, the more likely the IMAG-INATION is to "snap out" of whatever it has been doing, get to work, and turn the PICTURE into a reality for us. ❞**

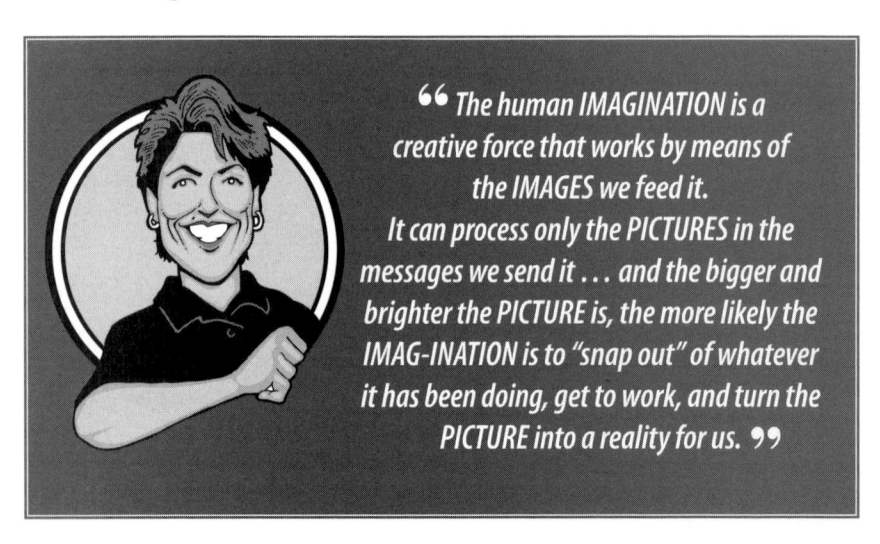

There is no possible way for the IMAG-ination to see a PICTURE that connects to negative words like "can't," "don't," and "avoid"! (To prove this to yourself, try holding a picture in your mind of the concept of "can't" – but be careful not to connect it to any other concept. What does "can't" look like?)

"I Can't see the word can't!"

Me neither! Nobody can!

But I'm not a visual person! I don't have a great imagination!

That's what you believe now. Brace yourself ...

Whatever you do...

> **DON'T THINK OF A JUICY,**
> **YELLOW, WEDGE OF LEMON ...**
> **DON'T THINK OF HOLDING IT HALF**
> **AN INCH ABOVE YOUR TONGUE ...**
> **DON'T THINK OF GETTING**
> **READY TO SQUEEZE THE LEMON**
> **ONTO YOUR TONGUE!**

> *Imagination is everything;*
> *it is the preview of life's coming attractions.*
>
> Albert Einstein

Do you still believe you "can't visualize"? If you read the words above, you now have evidence that you can visualize! Which belief serves you better?

That's what professional golfers do, by the way – they visualize as clearly as you just did. And the more you practice this, the better it gets.

THE POWER OF BELIEFS

What happens if we get very passionate about a message like "Don't hit the ball into the water"?

All the passion and color and power of that message is relayed to our IMAG-ination ... but since our IMAG-ination can't make a PICTURE of the word "Don't" – it settles for making a vivid, powerful PICTURE of the ball going into the water!

Thus, the message "Don't hit the ball into the water" turns into an IMAGE of THE BALL GOING INTO THE WATER! (By the way ... can you see the ball doing that right now? What happened to the word "DON'T?" IT VANISHED!)

Our brain focused on the water, and, what we focus on is always what we attract! (That's known as the Law of Attraction.)

The question then becomes ...

WHAT DO YOU WANT YOUR IMAGINATION TO ATTRACT?

If you're hooked on aggravation, you're going to find things that will aggravate you on the golf course... and in other areas of your life. Again: that's known as the Law of Attraction, and it is always in force. Thoughts attract like thoughts.

So. The first step is to become aware of what you currently believe. You must start noticing what you're thinking and what beliefs are driving the outcomes you are experiencing. Only by noticing and changing your beliefs will you attract what you need to improve both your internal and external performance.

> *Insanity is doing the same thing over and over again expecting different results.*
>
> Albert Einstein

Your beliefs are what you assume to be true about yourself and the world in which you live. They may have come about because of your own experiences, or because of the influence of important people in your life – parents, teachers, sports figures and role models. What you have to accept now is that *you* accepted these beliefs into your life. Take responsibility for that. You can change your beliefs — but as of right now, they are who you are, because you adopted them at some point.

A classic limiting belief on the golf course sounds like this:

"I always slice the ball on this hole."

>Or

"I always hit it out of bounds here."

>Or

"I always hit the ball in the water here. I better take my water ball out and use that one instead."

What happens when you pull out your "water ball" and use that ball instead? You've just reinforced a belief about golf that doesn't support you. You've just given yourself permission to hit the ball in the water!

I make a habit of taking all my mom's "water balls" out of her golf bag before we start playing. She no longer has any excuse to hit a second-rate ball into the water. Guess what? She hits the ball onto the green more often!

A classic limiting belief in larger life sounds like this:

"People always let me down."

>Or

"I'm just not good enough."

>Or

"I'm always late for appointments."

Your job is to replace limiting beliefs with empowering ones. Empowering beliefs sound like this:

"People are generally good hearted and mean well."

"I believe in myself and enjoy every moment I spend on the golf course."

"I see my golf game improving."

"My game is getting better and better every day."

Yes, these are "affirmations." Before you tell me that you don't believe in affirmations, consider this.

YOU ALREADY HAVE, AND ARE USING, A MYRIAD OF "AFFIRMATIONS" LIKE,

"I ALWAYS HIT THE BALL IN THE WATER!"

THEY'RE JUST NOT SERVING YOU VERY WELL!

Every time you think to yourself, "I'm a lousy putter," or "I always slice it here," you are using a negative affirmation to reinforce a belief that you have about yourself and your game. Take the time to replace those limiting affirmations with new, empowering affirmations – and start looking for, and creating, evidence to support the beliefs that are most useful to you. What matters is not whether any given belief you have about yourself and the world is "true." Let's face it — human beings can find evidence for just about anything!

To help you create new powerful Beliefs, refer to the Appendix I - Beliefs, for that Mind Power Stretching script.

One: Beliefs

The "Ah-haaaaaaaaaaaa" Moment.

TWO

AWARENESS

> *Only the day dawns to which we are awake.*
>
> Henry David Thoreau

What matters is whether you are choosing and reinforcing beliefs that are *useful to you.*

Awareness is the key to all constructive change. If we have not yet made the changes we want to make, on the golf course or anywhere else, it is because we have not yet become aware of the belief patterns that are currently holding us back.

This first "A" in your Baggage is almost the twin sibling to the element we discussed in the last chapter, Beliefs. What we believe affects what we are willing to notice; what we choose to notice tends to reinforce what we believe.

Once you understand your current patterns of belief, you are more likely to be able to take control of those patterns. If you are unaware of what your beliefs are, you will find yourself at the mercy of forces that "always" manage to keep you from performing at an optimal level on the golf course.

Does any of this sound familiar? Do you find yourself thinking things like, "I always have trouble with this hole?" And then wondering what strange force "makes" you land in the water on that hole, again and again?

Would you like to know what strange force that is?

It's not "bad luck." It's not the weather. It's not anything your opponent did.

Believe it or not, you do it to yourself.

That's the catch. You must become aware of what you are doing, because you are running this show. You unleash the "forces" that you may think you have nothing to do with, but that are actually the result of unsupportive ways of thinking you have developed over the years.

A CONVERSATION WITH YOURSELF

More often than you might expect, making an important change is as simple as asking yourself: "Okay, what are my beliefs?" ... and then listening attentively for the answer ... so you can become aware of what you believe.

So: You want to improve your swing, your score, your putting ability – whatever. In order to make that happen, you must be willing to start a conversation with yourself ... open yourself fully to that conversation ... and become truly aware of what that conversation reveals about you and your belief system.

BECOME AWARE OF THIS:

At any given moment, you are the sum total of what you believe and how you choose to act on those beliefs.

> **❝** *Your job right now is nothing more -- and nothing less — than to open a dialogue with yourself.*
> *In order to become aware of what you actually believe, you must make a conscious effort to notice your own internal dialogue on the golf course. You can tell whether or not you are making progress by how often you notice what you are saying to yourself, internally. How often, during your time on the golf course, do you stop yourself and think, 'Wow, I really just said that to myself!'?* **❞**

Think about the last time you played golf. Think back to a shot you hit that was so good, and the people you were playing with told you how wonderful the shot was. *What was your internal or verbal response to that event?*

Did you say, silently or out loud:

"Oh, that was just lucky."

        Or

"It really wasn't that good."

        Or

"I mis-hit it anyway."

If you apologized or put yourself down in any way, you need to become more aware of what you're saying to yourself.

CHANGE THE DIALOGUE

Most people go through life more or less unaware of the dialogue they're having with themselves. They may even think that they don't have an internal dialogue. Noticing that you do in fact have discussions with yourself is an essential precondition of changing that dialogue. ***The bottom line is — we all talk to ourselves, whether we can hear it or not!***

Perhaps, right now, your inner dialogue sounds like this:

"I always have a problem on this hole."

"My swing is terrible."

"I start out strong, but I can't seem to make the easy putts."

Stop and think. Are those really the kinds of beliefs you want to build your game around?

NOTICE YOUR PATTERNS

The reason it is so very important for you to notice your current patterns of belief is quite simple: You really will get what you focus on. That is true when you're on the golf course and when you're anywhere else. This is the Law of Attraction in action. And that law states that "like attracts like." What you think about, you will bring more of into your life. So: You must become aware of what you have been bringing to yourself.

Reality check: Becoming truly aware of your current belief patterns means becoming aware of how they were formed in the first place.

CONNECT THE DOTS

For most of the people I've worked with, developing awareness of belief patterns means "connecting the dots." It means noticing possible early family influences that have led to key feelings and beliefs. Be ready to "connect the dots." That does not mean you must go through months or years of therapy in order to improve your golf game! But it does mean …

YOU MUST BE WILLING TO NOTICE PATTERNS!

Be ready to become more aware of the most common, instinctive patterns you have built up. Ask yourself: How do I usually talk to myself during my golf game? How do I talk to others during my golf game? Does any of that match up with the way I talk to myself and others in other areas of my life? If the ways of seeing, feeling, and hearing yourself and your environment are not supporting you, it's time to replace those with better "programming."

The beautiful thing about awareness is that it makes it very easy for you to "reprogram" yourself. Awareness itself is therapeutic. The lack of awareness, by the same token, makes it difficult for you to change the patterns you're currently following – or to change the golf score that results from those patterns.

> " *You cannot expect to change anything that you are not aware of. It's impossible!* "

YOUR "CHECK ENGINE LIGHT"

Wouldn't it be great if we each had a "check engine light" in our brains that worked the same way the "check engine light" in our cars worked? Whenever there was a problem with our belief, the light would go on in our brains – and we'd pull over and check for trouble!

You do have a "check engine light" for your brain! It's called AWARENESS.

The minute you become aware — by asking yourself a question, like "What am I thinking right now?" – you're confirming the status of your mental "check engine light"! The simple act of asking yourself what you're thinking, will give you the answers you need. Once you build up the habit of asking yourself those kinds of questions, minute by minute, you will automatically know when your thinking is not supporting you.

> *Consciousness is nothing but awareness, the composite of all the things we pay attention to.*
>
> Deepak Chopra

TAKE CONTROL

Simple awareness can make it easier for you to process and move beyond painful incidents or relationships that may be lurking in your past. Once you become aware of what the pattern is right now, and why, you are in a much better position to take control of your golf game … and your life.

REALITY CHECK: *Yesterday does not determine today.*

Believe it! You really are free to build today exactly as you see fit.

- What you just did on the last hole does not determine how you're going to perform on this hole…unless you want it to.

- What you did when you were ten years old does not determine the options that face you when you are forty years old… unless you want it to.

You really can create this round of golf for yourself, today's round, exactly as you desire — if you are willing to become aware of what you believe and do, right now.

But in order for you to do that, you must master the art of talking to yourself. You must learn to talk to yourself in such a way that you and only you determine what happens in the conversation, and your responses to the larger world.

> **We all talk to ourselves. The trick is to become aware of what you're saying to yourself ... and to decide whether it is helping you or hurting you. If it is hurting you ... change what you're saying! You really do have that control.**

If you have learned to engage in unproductive ways of talking to yourself, unproductive ways of representing reality to yourself, unproductive conversations with others that you know don't serve you, you must notice these conversations so you can replace them with better ones.

THE AHA MOMENT

I was working with a golfer named Steve not long ago. As we made our way through the course, I asked him, "What do you like about your game?"

Steve said, "Well, I really *hate* the next hole!" And indeed he did. I could tell that he did, because his body language sent a sudden message of powerlessness and desperation the moment he raised the subject. His tone of voice, too, had changed.

I decided to ignore the fact that Steve had answered the question as though I wanted to find out what he didn't like. Instead, I simply said, "Okay – let's go play that hole. Let's take a look at this hole together. What do you think about it?"

"Well – at this point," Steve said, "I *always* hook the ball into the woods."

Where was he putting all of his imaginative power, all of his energy? On the belief that he would hook the ball into the woods! (By the way, here is a place to stop and think: What do you believe you ALWAYS do? Do you want to believe you ALWAYS do that?)

I asked Steve: "Okay – what do you WANT to do?"

"Well," he answered, "I *want* to hit it in the fairway."

"Fine," I said. "Let's analyze the fairway, analyze the hole. Let's look closely at where you want to come in from and what you actually want to do." We spent about ten minutes talking about what he wanted to do, instead of what he was already convinced he would always do.

I got Steve to understand that, if he took the time to notice what he was actually thinking, he would have control over what he decided to make big and bright in his world. It could either be the ball hooking into the woods or the ball landing on the fairway. But it couldn't be both. He had to pick one. And it was entirely up to him.

After I'd shared that, Steve said, "Wow — I never looked at it that way." We then did a short visualization technique. (You'll find the same technique set up for you to use in the Appendix of this book.) I asked, "What do you have to do to get the ball on the fairway? Can you see yourself doing that right now?"

And then an amazing thing happened. Steve got behind himself. He saw himself swinging with positive thoughts of what he wanted instead of what he didn't want.

In that moment, he got out of his own way.

He said: "Aha! THAT'S WHAT I WANT! I want to hit it over there."

The affirmation was, "I WANT!" (It replaced an affirmation he already had, an affirmation he had finally noticed and replaced. That old affirmation was called, "I hate this hole — I always hook the ball into the woods.")

Steve not only stopped hooking his ball into the woods, he started getting the ball into the middle of the fairway, just as he saw in his mind. He stopped the ritual of dreading that hole and actually looked forward to playing it!

CHANGING HIS PRINCIPLES FROM STATIC TO DYNAMIC

In the story I just shared with you, Steve went from static thinking (negative, closed off, and fearful) to dynamic thinking (positive, outgoing, and energized). It happened because he became more aware of what he wanted than what he didn't want. By creating a better picture in his mind, he changed his entire Baggage.

So – what do *you* want?

Reality check: You can learn to *re-focus* your thoughts and energy... *when you become aware!*

You must learn to focus on what you want rather than on what you don't want.

> *What your heart thinks is great, is great.*
>
> Ralph Waldo Emerson

Most of the people I work with find themselves creating a golf game that is not really a game at all, but more of a job. They say things like, "I'm just not enjoying it anymore. It feels like too much like work."

If it's not fun... stop and ask yourself the question...

"WHY AM I NOT HAVING FUN RIGHT NOW?"

If your golf game feels like work for you, you need to change the way you think ... which will change the way you feel. Changing the way you feel really will change your performance.

People sometimes think that they will feel better after they change the outcomes they experience for themselves. Actually, it's precisely the opposite. They will only get the good results they are looking for by finding ways to feel good before they do something. And that means changing their self-talk.

A student of mine, a teaching professional, was having problems with his short game. His internal self-talk was always focused on the difficulties he was having in this area. I told him that he wasn't going to change the outcome until he started to change his self-talk, visualize what he wanted, and start feeling good about chipping, pitching, and putting!

If you're not having fun, you're not playing up to your potential. You must move towards having fun!

A huge part of my job is to get people to notice when they're not having a good time on the golf course ... and notice what they could be feeling instead. Let me ask you this: Can you think of a time when you felt unsatisfied or frustrated with your golf game while you were out on the course?

If the answer is "yes," you should actually feel lucky. That was your mental and emotional system telling you that it's time to change the way you feel about your golf game. Once you learn to listen to that signal ... once you become aware of what your emotional state is ... you will find it very easy to move forward to a more supportive emotional state.

All too often, we talk ourselves out of believing that we're feeling unsatisfied or frustrated with the way things are going. We feel the "challenging" emotion ... but we don't accept that that's what we're actually creating and experiencing for ourselves.

> *One can overcome the forces of negative emotions, like anger and hatred, by cultivating their counter forces, like love and compassion.*
>
> Dalai Lama

FINDING YOUR INNER SWING WITH EMOTIONAL ENERGY

Think of your emotions, not just as "feelings" but as EMOTIONAL ENERGY. These energies show you what you are about to manifest of the golf course. They'll let you know if you're headed toward something that's going to mean sustained pain. They'll also let you know if you're heading toward something that will bring you sustained pleasure. Which would you rather experience?

Your emotions are like a smoke detector that beeps to let you know its batteries are low. A negative feeling, or emotion, is a warning signal that you must pay attention to! It's an indication that you're missing the connection to the highest, most empowering emotions – like love, gratitude and joy. This can change.

What I want you to notice right now is that, for most of us our emotions move up and down in sequence. We generally don't rocket from despair to a high sense of purpose within a period of thirty seconds. We don't plunge from joy to fear instantly.

> " *You work your way up or down.*
> *It's part of the human condition.*
> *That means you can notice where you are at any given moment. And once you've noticed where you are, you really can move up a step or down a step ...*
> *as you choose.* "

Take a look at the model on the following page:

Emotional Energy Ladder™

LOVE
GRATITUDE
JOY
PASSION
HAPPINESS
CONFIDENCE
OPTIMISM
HOPE
BOREDOM
IMPATIENCE
FRUSTRATION
WORRY
BLAME
ANGER
HATE
JEALOUSY
GUILT
FEAR

www.YourInnerSwing.com

Think of the process as climbing a ladder. Do you remember the old kids' game, "Chutes and Ladders?" That's what managing our emotional state is like. We're up at one level, and something happens, and then we slip down to a lower level. If we notice what has happened, we can figure out where we are – we can identify and become aware of the emotion we are feeling at any given moment. Once we are done with that emotion, we will be in a better position to identify what could happen next for us.

For instance, as I type out these words on my computer, I find myself feeling excited and enthusiastic about the countless people I am helping as I explain this process of managing emotional energy frequencies. That feeling of positive anticipation reminds me that I am close to the experience labeled "happiness" on the ladder.

Identifying where I am and where I could be next is a lot like ordering "happiness" from my mental "room service!"

Similarly, if I were to slip down the chute for some reason and find myself in the state labeled as *"frustration"* **the simple fact of noticing that this is where I am is the first step I need to take to move up, out of** *"frustration"* **and into** *"impatience" or "boredom."* I might even make a point of saying to myself, "Well, I'm feeling *frustrated* right now. *"Frustration"* isn't great, of course, but it's better than taking up full-time residence in the emotional state *"worry"* or *"blame."*

Little by little, step by step, if I notice where I really am, I can quickly move myself up the Emotional Energy Ladder™ to a more positive place, and ultimately feel better inside.

So – do you ever feel *"frustration"* out there? Are you willing to notice when you're feeling *"frustration"* – the very next time it happens?

Are you willing to work your way up the ladder, and assume personal responsibility for full awareness of your own emotional state? If so, I can guarantee you that you will have more fun ... perform better ... and post better scores.

> *Whatever the mind can conceive and believe, it can achieve.*
>
> Napoleon Hill

RE-AFFIRMING STATEMENTS

When you become aware of old belief patterns that no longer serve you, can create new ones that will. By repeating affirmations over and over the subconscious mind will remember and remind you, whether good or bad.

Read the statements below. Notice if any of them resemble your current golf thoughts. Use this activity to become aware of your own self-talk and to create a better conversation!

1. Negative affirmation: I don't want to hit it (out of bounds, in the water, in the sand) again.

Positive Affirmation: I imagine my shot landing on the (fairway, green).

2. Negative affirmation: I'll never be as good as (him, her).

Positive Affirmation: I enjoy playing to the best of my own ability.

3. This (driver, putter, wedge) is the worst. I hate this club!

Positive Affirmation: I love my (driver, wedge, putter) and love hitting good shots with it.

4. I hate this hole. I never do well on it.

Positive Affirmation: I love this hole! I enjoy the challenge of playing it well.

5. People will make fun of me when they see my score.

Positive Affirmation: I trust in my ability to play golf. I play the game for me.

6. I don't want to miss another three-footer.

Positive Affirmation: I have complete confidence in my stroke. My focus is on the target.

7. I am too (old, young, tall, small) to play good golf.

Positive Affirmation: I have every quality necessary to play golf well.

8. Golf is such a stupid game.

Positive Affirmation: I love the game of golf completely. I enjoy each experience I have on the golf course. Being outdoors, with people I love, getting exercise, and developing my skills makes it a great game!

9. I can't play well in the (wind, heat, cold).

Positive Affirmation: This is a great day for golf. I'm enjoying every moment.

10. I can't hit the ball as far as I want to.

Positive Affirmation: I am getting better with my distance and accuracy.

> *If any of the positive affirmations you read are helpful to you – be sure to write them down and keep them in your golf bag, so you can refer to them during your game!*

USING AFFIRMATIONS

A positive affirmation is an empowering thought that is repeatedly stated, read, written, or listened to with the goal of manifesting that thought. Athletes, corporate leaders, salespeople, and many other groups use positive affirmations to increase confidence and enhance performance.

Here are some of the best ways to use affirmations to build your awareness of your emotional state.

> **Commitment** - The key is being committed to your goal. Without a commitment to making the change or reaching your goal, affirmations are just words.
>
> **Repetition** - Repetition is the fuel that affirms success. Repeating positive statements replaces negative thoughts
>
> **Frequency** - Speak, write, or listen to your affirmation at least five to ten times in the morning and five to ten times in the evening.
>
> **Use first-person affirmations** - These take the form of you speaking passionately to yourself. (For example, "I am a great golfer.")

You know you're getting results when -

- The old thought, behavior, or performance disappears or lessens.

- Your mood, thinking, behavior, or performance changes in a positive direction.

- The old thought, behavior, or performance appears and your thinking immediately answers with the positive affirmation.

What to do

Use any affirmation stating what you want, deserve, or would like to happen in your golf game. For instance, "I deserve to win the tournament." Write it on a sheet of paper about 20 times.

How to Eliminate Negative Thoughts

Think and feel the words as you write them. Notice whether any doubt or negative thought accompanies what you are writing.

If this happens:

- Turn the paper over.

- Write down the negative thought that rebuts the affirmation. (For example, "I'm not playing well" or "There are too many players better than I am.")

- Write this down **ONCE** – not repeatedly.

- Then turn the paper back over and continue writing your positive affirmation.

When you have finished, look at the back of the sheet paper. This is your inner voice of self-doubt. This is what keeps you from creating and experiencing what you truly desire. Your subconscious mind will continue to remind you of the negative until you release it.

Here's how to release those negative thoughts:

- Write your affirming statement after each round of golf when all of your images and feelings are the strongest.

- Keep doing this exercise daily until there are no more negative thoughts regarding your affirmation.

- Write your positive affirmation on 3x5 cards or post-it notes. Place them where you will be constantly reminded of what you WANT.

To help you develop your new sense of Awareness refer to Appendix II - Awareness, for that Mind Power Stretching script.

The power of the mighty Gratitude Tee!

THREE

GRATITUDE

> *The direct experience of the consciousness of love is gratitude.*
> *Gratitude is the process of recognizing what is true.*
> *Gratitude is an act of awareness.*
> *Without awareness there is no love of anything.*
>
> Tae Yun Kim, Korean martial artist

Whenever I find that I am in an unsupportive emotional state, the simple act of finding something for which I can be grateful will almost always move me up to the next step on the Emotional Energy Ladder™. And it's so easy to find something to be grateful for! Just think of the food you eat, the air you breathe, the people who love you, and the unconditional love of a pet. It takes a fraction of a second to find something and express genuine gratitude for it.

The presence of gratitude brings into our lives MORE things to be grateful for. The absence of gratitude takes good things AWAY, minimizes opportunity, and makes us feel internally powerless – which, of course, impedes our performance on the golf course.

Gratitude is an essential part of any truly happy life. I don't care how much money you make, or what kind of car you drive, or what your job title is — if there is no gratitude in your life, you cannot be successful in any meaningful sense of that word.

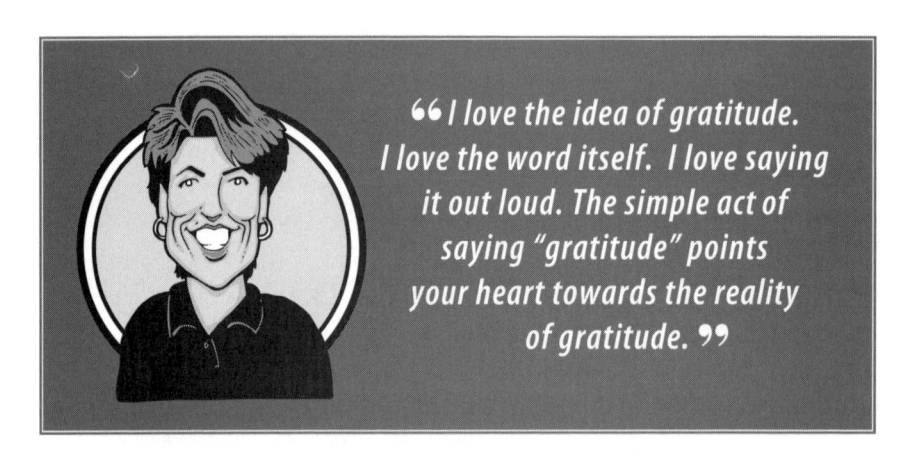

> *I love the idea of gratitude. I love the word itself. I love saying it out loud. The simple act of saying "gratitude" points your heart towards the reality of gratitude.*

Say it out loud right now!

"GRATITUDE!"

It's a beautiful word that can and will change the way you feel in an instant.

GRATITUDE, BLAME AND GOLF

Don't skip this section — it really is about golf!

Here's why. When you're not grateful, you're very likely to be in a "blaming" mindset. So, for instance, if you are thinking about something that your boss did wrong, or that your spouse did wrong, or that your teenaged son or daughter did wrong, this act of blaming will inevitably affect your mental preparation. And the "blame game" will definitely affect your golf game!

You cannot be in a grateful state and in a blaming or angry state at the same time. One emotion will always win out. If it's blame or anger, your score will suffer and you will lose out on a chance for personal growth. This is because blame deludes us into thinking that other people are responsible for our situation or our emotional state and keeps us from doing the kind of self-examination we need to move forward in our lives.

Suppose you say to your golfing partner: "I can't believe you made me miss that shot. No one can "make" you do anything or feel a certain way. How you feel is an inner emotion that you, and only you, have control of. Perhaps someone pushed your buttons and teased you, or maybe your teenage son didn't clean his room this morning. Even so, the way you respond to those events is entirely up to you. Remember, you always have the choice of what you think and how you feel. You hold the remote in your hands at all times. You can always change the channel.

> *No one can make you feel inferior without your consent.*
>
> Eleanor Roosevelt

Reality check: When we point the finger of blame at someone else ... three fingers always point back at us.

Gratitude has an amazing effect on human beings. For one thing, it instantly improves your body language and makes it easier for you to relax. I can always tell whether a person has a grateful state of mind on the golf course, just by watching their body language. The people who are grateful to be doing what they love, or grateful to be spending time with friends and family, or even grateful to have the time to be alone and experience the natural world – those people usually have better swings, and better body language than people who seem tense, blaming and frustrated.

The physicality of gratitude is obvious. Watch for grateful, relaxed body language in other golfers the next time you are out on the golf course. Use those golfers as your role models.

Gratitude opens you up to good things, because it opens up your heart. The lack of gratitude, on the other hand, tightens and constricts your body language, and shuts you down to the possibility of encountering good things. Feelings like jealousy, hate, anger and blame, close you down and bring more negativity into your life. Blame, in particular, is a powerful magnet for negativity.

It's very easy to blame others – too easy. Your job is to become aware of the Emotional Energy of blame when it occurs, so you can work your way up the Ladder and replace blame with gratitude.

Blame closes your heart. Our heart is the center of our soul and emotions. It's what guides us and brings us more of what is good in life. And the heart runs strongest on gratitude, not blame!

I believe that two of the highest emotions we can feel as human beings are love and gratitude. And I also believe that bringing gratitude into your world will lower your golf score! For now you're just going to have to trust me on this one. You'll see why soon enough!

Notice, though, that I'm not talking about simply making "mouth noise" in support of the idea of gratitude ... I'm talking about taking the time to be genuinely grateful for specific elements of your life. I'm talking about feeling that gratitude from the heart.

> *As we express our gratitude,*
> *we must never forget that the highest appreciation*
> *is not to utter words, but to live by them.*
>
> John F. Kennedy

For gratitude to move you upwards on the ladder, you have to literally feel gratitude from the heart. You have to feel it radiating inward and outward. You must first give gratitude if you wish to receive its benefits.

ARTHUR

Arthur was a slim eighteen-year-old who always seemed to be walking around the course with his head down and his shoulders slumped. He was a bit of a loner, usually keeping to himself on the range and on the course. Watching him hit balls I could tell that there was a great golfer just waiting to come out. I knew if I could show Arthur a way to a place of gratitude in his game he would appreciate how good he really was and could be.

One day, I was watching him hit balls and I walked up to him and said, "If you ever want to work on your game, let me know. I think you have a great swing with a lot of potential, and you could really be a solid golfer." Suddenly, Arthur's body language changed. He was suddenly energized and connected. The fact that I'd spoken to him, and complimented his game, gave him something positive to focus on. He reminded me of a four-year-old who had just been told he could have ice cream for breakfast!

For him, just that one unexpected change – the act of having the golf pro compliment his style – had a remarkable transformative effect.

In the days that followed, I focused on what he was doing right, kept giving him evidence in support of the idea of being grateful for the gifts he had been given as a golfer. I wasn't making any of this up, by the way. He really did have a natural, easy style. He just wasn't aware of it yet, and wasn't fully grateful for all that he'd been given. Every time I gave him a compliment, he would stare at me with wide eyes and ask, "Really? You really think so?"

And his game did improve, remarkably.

That same young man asked me how he could remember not to get down on himself, and how to stay in a positive grateful state when he hit a bad shot. I told him: "Every time you step onto the tee box with a golf tee in your hand, I want you to think of someone or something you are grateful for. It could be your health, your family, your friends, your ability to play golf. But you have to be grateful for something. You decide what it is."

> **YOUR GRATITUDE TEE**
>
> ❝ You can use the same tool as a reminder to enter — and stay in — a grateful state of mind. Every time you are on the tee box and take a tee out of your pocket... and every time you get ready to tee up your ball ... I want you to think of something that you are deeply grateful for.
> It may be the ability to provide for others, it may be your home, it may be the vacations you are able take, it may be your health, your family, or the air you're breathing. Learn to be grateful, and wonderful things will happen. ❞

Building up the habit of finding specific things for that young man to be grateful for wasn't the only thing I did with him, but I think it was the most important thing. I was a sounding board for him. As we chatted, and as I made comments on his game and his life, I was always finding ways to give him more evidence for feeling good about himself, or feeling grateful for where he was, for feeling happy about what he had inside of himself and what he was doing.

That's all I want you to do right now. Keep looking for evidence in support of the idea, "I choose to be grateful." Keep focusing on the many, many gifts you've been given. They really are limitless.

Do you have:

• Air to breathe?

• Good food to eat?

• Friends and family who support you?

• Clean clothes to wear?

Keep being grateful for those gifts that we so often take for granted. When you continue to picture, feel, hear and acknowledge everything you have, doors will open to limitless possibilities for you.

NOTICE WHAT YOU NOTICE

When gratitude vanishes, it typically does so because your mind has identified and attached itself to some perceived "problem." If there's no particular challenge for your mind to focus on in your present-tense world as you're golfing, you may reflect on some perceived difficulty that happened in the past, or you may anticipate some obstacle you could face in the future.

It's quite common for our attention to settle on "problems" in this way. As adults, most of us have gotten used to paying attention to past, present, and future challenges almost by default. Unfortunately, we can develop a "problem-focused" habit of attention in which we are so busy identifying things that don't support us that we fail to notice the many things that do support our existence – our health, our work, our family, our energy, our ability to focus on the things we want to do, — I could give you hundreds of other examples. The more the "habit of attention" has developed to focus on our perceived "problems," the less likely we will be able to experience gratitude.

> **"** *There are no "problems" – there are only challenges and opportunities. The words you use to describe things really do matter! Hitting the ball over the water is a challenge ... not a problem! Resolve right now to remove the "P" word from your internal and external vocabulary.* **"**

You can change your habit of attention by changing your internal observations. Take ten minutes and write down, without interruption, all the things you can think of that you have received from other people. Do it now. Creating this list with full attention will surprise you ... and change your outlook on life.

When I stepped back from my life and began quietly reflecting on everything that had been done for me and given to me, I was surprised — and overwhelmed — by the sheer volume of gifts that I had received in my life. By making a list of these gifts, I felt more cared for, more loved, and more supported than ever before. I learned to notice gifts I had not been noticing before. Noticing those gifts is an art, and it does require some practice, but fortunately it's pretty easy to master, and the results are amazing.

OBSTACLES TO GRATITUDE

Let's consider now three of the greatest obstacles to gratitude:

---

1. Self-preoccupation

2. Taking gifts for granted

3. Sense of entitlement

---

1. Self-preoccupation

When we are preoccupied with our own thoughts, feelings, and needs, we often have very little attention left over to notice all the things that are being done to support us. Think of your attention as a flashlight. As long as you shine the light on your troubles, difficulties, aches and pains, there will be no light available for you to see what other people are doing for you.

2. Taking Gifts for Granted

When I press the switch on my bedside lamp, I assume the light will go on. Indeed, the vast majority of the time, it does go on! Once I've come to expect something, the gift doesn't usually get my attention each time I receive it. In fact, my attention doesn't come into play at all … until my expectation isn't met! Translation: I may only notice that the light bulb has burned out … and forget to take into account all the work and effort necessary to invent the incandescent light bulb, or the convenience of having a bedside lamp as opposed to a candle. When I take gifts for granted, it is easier for me to feel ungrateful about them, or even to resent their temporary absence.

3. Sense of Entitlement

This connects with the idea of taking gifts for granted, but is focused in a powerful way on what we believe we "have coming" to us. The more I think I've earned something or deserve something, the less likely I am to feel grateful for it. As long as I think I'm entitled to something, I won't consider it a gift.

> *The aim of life is appreciation; there is no sense in not appreciating things; and there is no sense in having more of them if you have less appreciation of them.*
>
> G. K Chesterton, English Poet

DEVELOPING A PRACTICE

To feel a sense of heartfelt gratitude, we must overcome those three obstacles. Self-reflection provides the path for us to do so. It allows us to pause and appreciate what is being given to us ... rather than focus on what we don't have. Through self-reflection, we can see everything we do have, and all that we are, as gifts.

Many people don't truly appreciate all they have until it is gone. Being truly grateful is sharing your appreciation today. Otherwise, tomorrow has little meaning.

The gratitude – or lack of gratitude – you feel in your life depends on what you practice. For example, complaining is a wonderful practice to develop if you wish to cultivate disappointment, resentment and self-pity. If you've ever tried this practice, you may have noticed that it's quite effective. Each time you complain, you get better at complaining, and you draw more things into your life to complain about. It's like learning to play an instrument. Practice really does make perfect – so be very careful what you practice!

Without practice, there can be no development of any skill. Without practice, there is only the idea of developing that skill. You cannot become a grateful person just by thinking that you want to be grateful at some point in the future. You can't just say "I'm grateful." You must do something to make gratitude a reality in your life.

To get on the "frequency" of gratitude, we need to develop a new habit of attention. We need to notice the concrete ways in which the world supports us each and every day. Only then can we develop new habits of attention, speech, and action – and start expressing our gratitude to others.

Start your gratitude practice today: **Observe. Reflect. Express.**

> *Hey, what's that sound? Oh, it's the alarm on my cell phone reminding me I have an appointment. What a nice feature. It frees up my mind to attend to other things. Thanks, cell phone. And thanks to my sister who gave it to me. And thanks to all the people who made it. And thank goodness my finger works well enough to shut it off!*

AMY, GRATITUDE, AND THE CLUB CHAMPIONSHIP

I first met Amy at her country club, when she came to one of my Golf Mind Power Workshops. At 15 years old, she was physically and mentally mature beyond her years. She was already hitting the ball much farther than most girls her age, and mentally she was open to receiving new strategies for developing her mind power in order to play golf at a higher level.

My workshops help people get out of their own way by realizing that mind power comes from within. I teach the power of the "GLO" principle and how to start the day with life-giving vibrations. It's the idea that Gratitude, Love and Opportunity will raise your Emotional Energy — and improve your performance throughout the day. My students take home a statement to read out loud, with emotion, in the moment just after waking up, even before their feet touch the floor.

Here it is:

> **"What a glorious day to feel Gratitude, Love and Opportunity!"**

(Say that tomorrow morning… with emotion!)

Amy used the **GLO** principle to help her win her first tournament… a club championship, which she later told me was a very important win for her on many levels. We had one or two conversations before her event in which I reminded her to be grateful for her wonderful ability to play in the championship; I reminded her to enjoy the process of competing in it as a journey. I also reminded her to love every hole, every shot, and every putt. Finally, I reminded her that the greens were going to be the perfect speed … just for her.

Here's part of my e-mail correspondence with Amy:

> *Hi Randy -*
> *It's Pam and me in the final round match play for the ladies' club championship. I've been using your putting strategies and imagined the ball in the cup. It helped most of the time. Also… what do you suggest to think when you're not playing well to do better on the next hole? Because, sometimes it feels like one hole can ruin it for me. Thanks a lot!*
>
> *Amy*

Amy,

That is so great! I am proud of you sticking with the creative visualization techniques we worked on. Believe it or not, I was at a PGA Event earlier this week working with a touring professional on his visualization. You see, even the top players in the world work on this important mental aspect to better their physical performance. So stick with it.

As for not playing well… remember to stay in the present. It's a one shot at a time game. Instead of saying to yourself, "I am not playing well," say "I am patient and focused on one shot at a time." If a shot goes a stray, let that shot (or hole) go, get back into play and get the ball in the hole. STAY FOCUSED ON YOUR GOAL AND GAME PLAN and HAVE FUN!

Randy, thanks for returning my email. I'm so excited for tomorrow and nervous at the same time. Everyone's watching and wants me to win!

Ahhhh...I'll keep you updated on how it goes,

Amy

Amy,

Remember "GLO... What a glorious day to feel Gratitude, Love and Opportunity all around me." Enjoy the experience of the day and let things happen!

Hey Randy... I WON!!!!

It was amazing

I was down 2 holes after 6 holes and then straight up won holes 7 - 14!

I was dormy after 13... and all I had to do was tie the 14th to win...

but instead I knocked in a 40 ft putt from off of the green!!! Like you taught me, I saw it and rolled it in! It was amazing... Pam was a great competitor but it definitely feels so good to win! :) Thanks for all of your help,

Amy

In order to succeed, your desire for success should be greater than your fear of failure.

Bill Cosby

FOUR MONTHS LATER ...

The story gets even better. Four months later, Amy called me in a panic. She was in an International Junior Event and had just finished the first day having shot 90. Her game was physically better than a 90, and she knew it... she just didn't know what to do to get out of her own way.

During our phone session, Amy told me all about the round and how she shot the 90. We both realized right away that what she was facing was not a physical issue, but instead a mental block – a case of Amy not letting inner trust in her own abilities happen. She knew she had become afraid of all the things that "might happen" when she swung. Since I happened to be in south Florida, near where she was playing, I met with her the next day. We worked on a more solid pre-shot routine which gave her the confidence and freedom to use her visual skills to guide her. We also targeted a goal of shooting 80, a score she said would make her very happy.

To help her relax, I did a relaxation session with her that was focused on allowing gratitude to surround her golf game. (You'll find similar exercises for you to use in the Appendix of this book.) I told Amy to see herself playing golf at a beautiful ocean view course, and to realize just how blessed she was. The relaxation session was based around loving herself, enjoying the moment, and then anchoring that wonderful feeling to the next round of golf she played. I told her to enjoy every moment and every challenge presented to her in the round coming up. As the session closed, I told her simply to let the round happen and go with the flow of the day. Whatever happened, it would all be good.

When we spoke that night, Amy was ecstatic. She had shot an 83, which was big improvement from the 90 she'd shot the day prior — and she had only missed her goal score by a few shots!

Even the way Amy explained her round to me was exciting. When she told me she shot a ten over par 47 on the front nine, you would have thought she shot a 27! Her attitude had made a 180 degree turn from the day before. Everything was okay now. Why? Because she had managed her own emotions for the entire day. She was still in the "attitude of gratitude." It was her gratitude, her sense of enjoying the day, that had made every shot and every hole fun.

If you don't have a goal … how will you know where you're going?

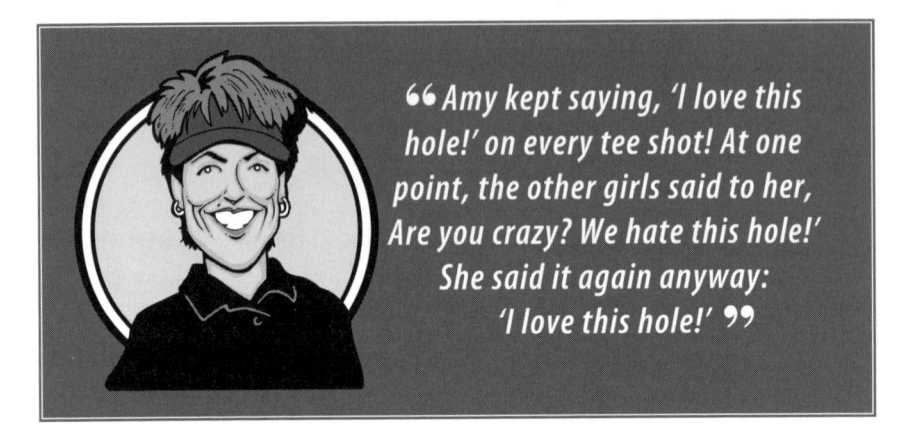

> **Amy kept saying, 'I love this hole!' on every tee shot! At one point, the other girls said to her, 'Are you crazy? We hate this hole!' She said it again anyway: 'I love this hole!'**

To help you cultivate a higher state of Gratitude refer to Appendix III - Gratitude, for that Mind Power Stretching script.

Three: Gratitude

Right on target.

FOUR

GOALS

> *My ability to concentrate and work toward the goal has been my greatest asset.*
>
> Jack Nicklaus

It's like driving across the country without a destination, without a map, without any directions, and without even a compass. You'll be going somewhere, of course. You'll be on a journey, but you'll have no destination. If you ever find yourself getting dizzy from "driving in circles," this chapter will help.

WHAT DO YOU WANT?

The very first question I always ask my student is "What do you want?"

Often, because they don't know what they want, I hear silence. Although most golfers are aware of what they **don't** like and have plenty to complain about in their game, they're not sure what they actually **do** want. They have no direction because they have no goal.

Setting the right goals gives you focus.

So…

1. What do you want?
2. Do you have a current goal?
3. What would you like to improve in your game?
4. Could you describe what you'd like to improve in your golf game to me or to anyone else?
5. How could you use a description of what you want to do and build a positive goal statement for yourself?
6. Lastly, *when* exactly, would you like to accomplish your goal?

When I ask people "What do you want?" or "What's missing in your game?" I typically hear answers like this:

"Well, I always screw up on the eleventh hole."

Or
"I can't chip the ball without skulling it over the green."

Or
"I can never break 100."

These are good starting points — they show that you are aware of what you can't do or what you are doing that you don't like. **But** …they're not yet goals.

Goals should inspire you, excite you, and get you to take action! Look at the statements on the previous page. Do any of them sound familiar to you? If so, see how you can revise the wording with positive intention of what you want, and when you want to make that happen.

> *Man is a goal-seeking animal. His life only has meaning if he is reaching out and striving for his goals.*
>
> Aristotle

THREE GREAT THINGS GOALS DO

Goals help focus your attention and point your mind in a specific direction. With the right goal in mind, you automatically become more focused on goal-relevant activities, and you automatically move away from actions that don't support you or aren't relevant to the goal.

Goals create efficient effort by giving you a sense of purpose. Situation one: You work on chipping by going to the green and hitting chips haphazardly for 30 minutes, without a target. Situation two: you chip for 30 minutes with the clear purpose of getting five balls within five feet of the hole. In the second situation, you spend your time much more efficiently – because you have a purpose guiding your half hour of practice time.

Goals influence persistence. They inspire us to keep reaching. We tend to continue just a little bit longer, make our effort a little bit stronger, and be a little bit happier when we have the right goal. We tend to strive instead of strain.

PUT YOUR GOAL INTO WORDS

What would your goal sound like if you turned it into a single sentence? It might sound like this:

I am in the process of improving my game to the point where I can routinely break 100, which I plan on doing for the first time by September 1st of this year.

An affirmation in support of this goal would sound something like this:

I break 100 easily and frequently!

If you aren't willing to create a statement about what you are hoping to accomplish next on the golf course, and an affirmation that supports it, then you are still carrying around static Baggage that is keeping you from growing and performing up to your potential on the golf course.

Don't make the mistake of believing you can "just get by on enthusiasm." You can't. *You must have a clear goal* that re-energizes you and points you in a specific direction. Your enthusiasm will dissipate if you don't. I work with many people who are extremely goal-oriented in certain parts of their lives … but somehow miss the importance of setting goals on the golf course.

I also work with people who have difficulties when it comes to setting goals in just about any area of their lives. Usually this is because they've never set any meaningful goals for themselves at all.

In either situation, the basic question you must ask yourself is the same: What do you want? If your answer is, "I'm really not sure yet," (or any variation), there's a follow-up question for you to consider:

HOW LONG ARE YOU WILLING TO SPEND YOUR TIME WITHOUT HAVING A CLEAR PURPOSE?

If you are in any way disillusioned about the process of setting a goal for yourself ... if you have any negative associations that relate to goals you established in the past that ended up looking too lofty and unrealistic ... I have good news for you. *It's not your fault!*

If there was a problem in the past with your goal orientation, the only possible explanation is that you somehow hooked up with a goal that didn't inspire you.

The goals we select for ourselves *must* energize us and excite us. That's the job of a goal! *Our* job is simply to find the goal that instantly feels right, instantly puts us in a positive frame of mind.

If we ever lose sight of the goal, ignore it, or start "hoping" we reach it, the problem is not that we're bad people, but rather that we *haven't yet picked the goal that really connects.* That's okay. We just have to keep looking!

> You can find the right goal ... and then find ways to measure how close you're actually getting to fulfilling it. The key to pulling this off is *simply realizing that it is okay to change and modify your goal along the way.*

Sometimes, modifying your goal is the best thing you could possibly do. It shows that you're paying attention and moving in the direction you want to go.

> *If you want to reach a goal, you must 'see the reaching' in your own mind before you actually arrive at your goal.*
>
> Zig Ziglar

GOALS MUST BE QUANTIFIABLE

It's not enough to say, "my goal is to improve my swing," or "my goal is to be a better golfer." Those goals fail to connect on any emotional level, and they are impossible to measure!

- How will you *know* when your swing has "improved?"
- How will you *know* when you have become a "better golfer?"
- What will you be measuring?

When you set a goal, quantify it! Create a goal that allows you to acknowledge that you have actually reached the finish line. When you shoot 99 for the first time, you will know for sure that you have reached your goal of "breaking 100!" (And, by the way, when you do hit your goal, celebrate!)

BUILD "DO" GOALS

I always tell my students to put their goals in a positive voice, and to steer clear of any goal that sounds negative, or that uses the words "don't," "can't," or "stop" prominently.

Your goal must make a request from "room service" that you really want to make. In the case of a statement like ***"I don't want to hit the ball in the water,"*** you should ask yourself: What will your internal "delivery system" see – and then deliver to you?

Look closely at the words in that sentence again, and pick out the words that will create a picture in your mind. Ready?

I…hit … ball .. water.

That's all you could possibly get your **IMAG**ination to visualize!

Hit more balls in the water, please! Since there is no image for the word "don't," the picture you will you see is "ball going into the water."

Putting the goal statement into the positive voice would sound like this:

"I want to hit more fairways and greens."

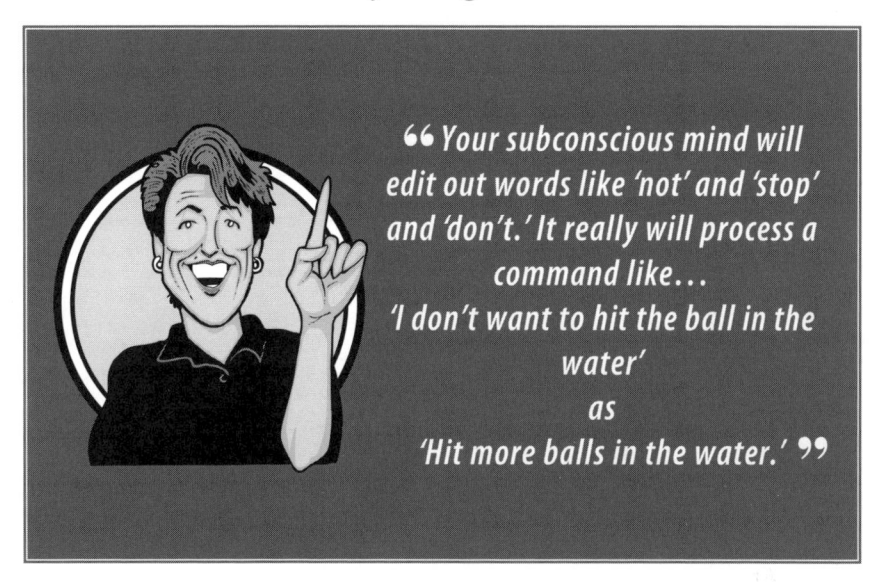

> **Your subconscious mind will edit out words like 'not' and 'stop' and 'don't.' It really will process a command like...**
> **'I don't want to hit the ball in the water'**
> **as**
> **'Hit more balls in the water.'**

The Law of Attraction will always bring you more of what you asked for. You saw the ball going in the water ... you projected the image of hitting more balls in the water. Unless your goal is built around the picture you want – namely, hitting more fairways and greens — you will get more balls going into the water!

When you connect with the right goal, get specific about it, and start thinking about it on a regular basis, you will find that you get excited about why it is imperative for you to achieve it!

IF YOUR GOAL IS TO LOWER YOUR HANDICAP, THEN GET SPECIFIC ABOUT THAT GOAL!

By how much do you want to lower your handicap?
By what point in time?
Why is it important for you to lower your handicap?
How will you feel when you've lowered your handicap?

Is your goal to understand your own game better?
How will you know when this has happened?
What are the benchmarks, specifically?
What is your time frame to hit those benchmarks?
Why is this goal important to you?
How will you feel when you achieve this goal?

Do you want to become a better putter?
How much better?
Do you want to two-putt more 30-footers?
Do you want sink more five-footers?
Do you want to have 36 putts per round or fewer?
By what date do you want to accomplish this?

WRITE IT DOWN!

CREATE SMART GOALS

Here is where the rubber hits the road. On the next page, write down two or three golf-related goals that you want to achieve. Look at each goal and **evaluate** it. Make any changes necessary to ensure it meets the criteria for a **SMART goal.**

A SMART goal is simply ….

S = SPECIFIC

M = MEASURABLE

A = ATTAINABLE

R = REALISTIC

T = TIME-FOCUSED

1. *Specific.* Unclear goals produce unclear results. Specific goals are easier to reach than general ones. For example, a general goal would be to hit more fairways. But a specific goal would be to get the right driver, take a lesson every other week that shows me how to hit more fairways, and practice with my driver three days a week.

2. *Measurable.* This means that you set goals that you can measure. Your goals should be such that you know how much you have accomplished and how much further you still have to go. For example, knowing that you hit two fairways the last time you played gives you a starting point to create a measurable goal the next time you play.

3. *Attainable.* It's important to set realistic goals. If right now, you're hitting the driver 150 yards, it would not be a realistic goal to aim for hitting 300 yards by next week. That kind of goal will only frustrate you. Goals should not be out of your reach, yet they should challenge you enough that you actually have to stretch to reach them.

4. *Realistic.* Goals must represent something you're truly willing to work at. Your goal to start hitting drives of 200 yards will be realistic — if you think it is attainable.

5. *Time-focused.* One of the most powerful aspects of a great goal is that it has a definite time frame. You should know by what point in time you want to hit drives of 200 yards. If the time limit expires, and you haven't yet hit the goal, you can re-evaluate and set a new goal.

Go for it! Write your SMART goal in the space below!

My Goal: _____

_____

_____

_____

Now that you have developed a written goal that inspires you, you can build some affirmations into your daily routine that will strengthen your goal-setting muscle in the long term. For instance:

- I create goals that help me stretch beyond my limitations.
- My goals help me improve my golf game in every way.
- I choose SMART goals that I write down and read daily.
- My goals drive me to improved thoughts, feelings and emotions.
- I love setting goals that improve my golf.
- I love to accomplish my goals and create more goals.
- I am a goal setter in golf and life.

If reading this list inspires you to create affirmations of your own related to setting goals … go ahead and write them down … and leave them in a place where you can look at them or add to them at least once a day.

YOUR GIFT TO YOU

Setting the right goals means creating what you really want to do in your own world. This ability to create a goal that motivates you is a gift for you, from you. Celebrate that gift! Remember, if this process isn't enjoyable for you, you can always change the process.

Once you attain a goal, your job is, of course, to celebrate … and then set a new goal! In the Appendix of this book, you'll find a special relaxation exercise that will help you set newer and better SMART goals that are custom-created for your world.

> *Setting goals for your game is an art.*
> *The trick is in setting them at the right level,*
> *neither too low nor too high.*
>
> — Greg Norman

> *By recording your dreams and goals on paper, you set forth in motion the process of becoming the person you most want to be.*
>
> Mark Victor Hansen

If you can't (or won't) put your goal down on paper, you haven't got a goal. You only have a wish.

"I wish I were a better putter."

"I wish I could keep it in the fairway."

"I wish I scored better."

These are not goals. They're wishy-washy dreams.

AREN'T YOU READY FOR MORE THAN JUST A WISH?

Writing your goal down is an essential first step. Once you can write it down, you can internalize it by reading it at the beginning and end of each day. In this way, you can make the goal *real* for yourself within your mind and body. The goal will become part of who you are. What you want most on the golf course will be obvious to you. What you are moving toward will be obvious to you, no matter what happens.

Until you get something you can put down on paper and measure your performance against, it's all talk. You are not yet activating the powerful "I want" muscle that lies waiting within your mind.

Setting the right goal can get you over any hurdle! You can conquer fear of success, fear of public speaking, fear of anything ... *when you set a plan in motion that motivates you!* If you are doing that properly, the fear will vanish!

"Your wish is *YOUR* command."

FEAR OF GOAL SETTING

Do you know why most people don't write down goals? Because it makes them accountable. Accountability is responsibility! And sometimes, responsibility is scary.

Let me ask you this though: Isn't it more scary when no one is responsible for the outcomes in your life?

> HAVE YOU REACHED THE POINT YET WHERE IT'S ACTUALLY SCARIER NOT TO HAVE A GOAL?

Every great golfer I've ever worked with had a goal to achieve. Each one of them knew that the bar could be raised just a little higher in their game ... by setting a new goal.

Whatever you do, don't play your next game of golf without a goal. Identify something concrete that you want to accomplish by the end of the round! It may be as simple as keeping the stats of how many fairways you hit, or how many putts you had.

Set a goal that makes you stretch, even if it's small! Replace the old commercial you have been playing:

"I've never been able to break 90"

— with a new one:

"My goal is to break 90 on or before August 1st."

Make it positive. Give it a deadline. Know where you're going!

You have to set goals that are almost out of reach. If you set a goal that is attainable without much work or thought, you are stuck with something below your true talent and potential.

Steve Garvey

Setting a goal is like growing a garden: you must first turn the soil and plant the seed. That's like having a short-term goal. Then you have to tend the garden over time: That's like having a long-term goal. Nothing truly wonderful is going to sprout up overnight. You must enjoy the process as well as the final outcome.

BOB

I was working with Bob; he had a tournament coming up in two weeks. His goal was to "shoot low enough to get into the next round."

I said, "Okay, Bob, I hear you, but I think we need to get more specific. What do you think you need to shoot to get in?"

He said, "I'd probably have to shoot an 80 to play into the next round."

I said, "Tell you what — lets make it 78. That gives us little leeway of a few shots. Let's write it down." So we did. I made sure he wrote out his goal of shooting 78 and getting into the next round of the tournament as a result.

Then we did a relaxation session. After we were done, I asked him to keep reinforcing in his mind the score he wanted: 78. I told him it wasn't important how he was going to shoot 78 — his job was just to look at that number now and then and build it into his day using a positive, expectant, confident state of mind.

I didn't hear from him for couple of weeks. Then I got phone call from him.

He said, "Randy, I still can't believe what happened." He seemed reluctant to speak somehow.

> *Shoot for the moon. Even if you don't get there, you'll be among the stars.*
>
> Franklin D. Roosevelt

"Why, Bob? What's the matter?"

"There's nothing wrong," he answered. "I just can't believe what I have to tell you. You're never going to believe what I just shot in that tournament."

"Oh, I don't know — maybe I will."

"Randy," he said, "do you remember the number we wrote down that I was supposed to shoot? It was 78 — and I shot a 78! It absolutely blew my mind. I still can't believe that I was able to perform at that level in this kind of competition. I moved on – I made it into to the next tournament! I just called to say 'Thank you.'"

I love those phone calls! I love it when people set goals, get better at believing in themselves, and get out of their own way.

> To help you create powerful new Goals refer to
> Appendix IV - Goals, for that Mind Power Stretching script.

**If you want to discover someone's true attitude . . .
go play golf with them!**

FIVE

ATTITUDE

> *Nothing can stop the man with the right mental attitude from achieving his goal; nothing on earth can help the man with the wrong mental attitude.*
>
> Thomas Jefferson

Have you ever noticed that critical business alliances and brilliant career connections that last a lifetime are often formed during a four-hour round of golf? Have you noticed that, by the same token, many business deals fall apart before the players even get to the back nine?

Why do you think that is?

I'll share my answer to that important question with you a little later on in this chapter.

WHO STANDS OUT?

I would like you to think about one person you know well from any period in your life, whether you've played golf with that person or not. Think of someone who stands out in your mind as having a truly great attitude — someone who is always looking "on the bright side" of things.

Have you got that person in mind right now? Great.

Was there a person who came to mind instantly? If not, keep thinking until you come up with a teacher, a close relative, a coworker, or a friend from your past whose outlook on life is or was bright and upbeat. When you can see that person's face in your mind ... keep reading.

This inherently optimistic person you're thinking of right now... how did you feel about them personally? Did you (or do you) like and respect the individual as a person, and enjoy spending time with him or her?

My guess is that you *do* enjoy this person's company. Most of us look forward to interactions with people who consistently have "good attitudes," people who are willing to assume the best about any situation they encounter — or at least not assume the worst. We find them enjoyable to be with *because they are a source of positive energy and emotions* – and we like to build those feelings into our own lives. People like this make us feel good. Often, we say things about them like:

- "He's a born optimist."
- "She's got a sunny disposition."
- "Nothing ever seems to get her down – she's got this natural ability to bounce back."

Here's my question for you: Would you like to *be* one of those people? It's easier than you may think.

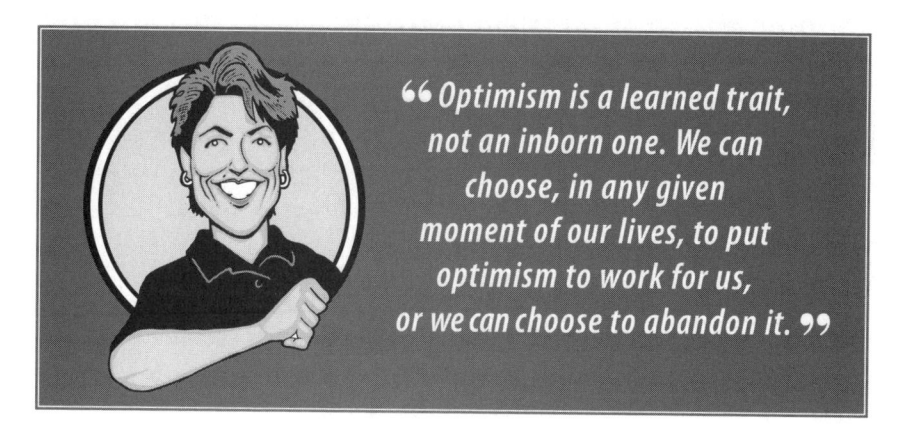

> **Optimism is a learned trait, not an inborn one. We can choose, in any given moment of our lives, to put optimism to work for us, or we can choose to abandon it.**

Sure – it's easier for some people to look on the bright side than it is for other people. But with just a little effort everyone can learn to be more optimistic about life… and the way you feel about your golf game is an excellent place to start. In fact, to my way of thinking, it's the very best place to start.

The question is – what kind of evidence are you looking for?

Are you looking for evidence that your game is going well? Are you looking for evidence that you are learning from and enjoying the experience? Are you looking for evidence that you are fortunate in being able to spend time doing something that you enjoy … or could enjoy?

Or …

Are you perhaps looking for evidence that your game is going poorly? That you "always" make the same mistakes? That you are "unfortunate" when it comes to the "breaks" you receive on the links?

> *Any fact facing us is not as important as our attitude toward it, for that determines our success or failure. The way you think about a fact may defeat you before you ever do anything about it. You are overcome by the fact because you think you are.*
>
> — Norman Vincent Peale

"IN THE FLOW"

Maybe you've heard people talking about a golf game where everything was clicking, where they felt themselves to be "in the flow" or "in the zone." Would you like to play that kind of game, regularly? Your *attitude* is what will make that possible – or impossible – for you to do so.

There really is a sublime current you can follow that creates a dynamic pattern of success and optimism. But here's the catch: If you want to follow that current, you have to choose the attitude you live in. You have to choose what your attitude is going to be about your game, and you have to choose what your attitude about your larger life is going to be.

> *The way you look at yourself and the world at large determines whether you are "in the flow" or not.*

THE SEVEN-SECOND ASSESSMENT

Why is this important? Consider this. When you meet someone for the first time, it takes that person between three and seven seconds to make a judgment about you. Human beings decide pretty quickly whether a given person is worth getting close to, worth letting into their "circle." People will make that seven-second decision about you based on things like tonality, eye contact, body language and other factors … all of which will add up to an instant, intuitive assessment of your attitude.

In other words, other people's perceptions of you and conclusions about you are going to happen quickly ... and they are going to be driven by perceptions of your attitude! Nowhere is this more true than on the golf course.

Reality check: Your attitude invariably affects your game, because attitude and energy go hand in hand.

> *Your attitude at any given moment is the visible manifestation of your current beliefs about yourself and the world you live in.*

I'm repeating it so you can read it again!

Your attitude at any given moment is the visible manifestation of your current beliefs about yourself and the world you live in.

BEYOND COMPARTMENTALIZING

You can tell a lot about a golfer's attitude toward life just by the way that person interacts with others on the course.

Invariably, the people who do compartmentalize their world – for instance, to have one kind of attitude with me, the golf pro, but another more aggressive or disrespectful attitude toward the caddy – are the ones who have the biggest problems with their game. Some senior executives I've worked with fall into that category; they seemed out of balance somehow. Their attitude is the reason for that. They can "pull the trigger" on a big business deal … but they can't seem to "pull the trigger" that lowers their golf score. Why? Regardless of their external level of success, their beliefs create a self-defeating attitude that is based on winning self-esteem by reducing the self-esteem of others. This attitude is what holds them back.

On the golf course, there is no place to hide. Your true self is on display. Your real attitude toward yourself and the opportunities and obstacles you face is obvious for anyone who cares to notice. It's *you* in the spotlight – the *real* you.

> *I love the man that can smile in trouble,*
> *That can gather strength from distress,*
> *And grow brave by reflection.*
>
> — Thomas Paine

WHAT CEOS KNOW

By the way – the fact that your true self is on display on the golf course brings us to the answer to the question I asked you at the outset of this chapter. That question was: Why are so many important business deals either sealed, or abandoned, on the golf course?

It's because, when you play golf with someone, that person's attitude and personality becomes obvious. That's what CEOs know. They want to figure out who people really are and how they handle themselves under pressure — as opposed to who people say they are. There is no faking that on the golf course. So – smart CEOs take potential business allies out for a game of golf ... so they can find out who they're really dealing with?

Sometimes we live under a delusion. The delusion is that we have a couple of different lives we can live, and that we can choose which compartment we are going to occupy at any given moment. We think we can be one person to the salesman, another person to our boss, and yet another person to our spouse or significant other.

GOLF STRIPS ALL THAT AWAY. IT SHOWS EVERYONE WHO WE REALLY ARE.

During a game of golf, your true attitude, your true *self*, is on display. This raises an important question:

> *Are you willing to notice your attitude, and the self it reveals, and decide whether that's who you really want to be?*

You might as well know now. When you step out on the golf course, you are naked. You are unprotected and on display. You are sharing all your secrets with the world. You are running naked down the fairway – and exposing yourself with every swing. You can't camouflage anything. You can't possibly "fake it." You are who you are.

YOUR GAME IMPROVES ... AS YOU DO

Your game will not get any better if you don't consciously choose the attitude you want to bring to the course. Your game will not improve until you "lift up" the thoughts that create that attitude. Believe it: **You aren't going to be able to improve your game in any meaningful way until you also commit to growing and improving as a person.**

WHAT DOES YOUR GOLF ATTITUDE SAY ABOUT YOU?

Does your attitude on the golf course make you say or think things like this?

- Look at that shot. She gets all the breaks!
  - I never get any breaks!
- I can't believe how hot it is today!
  - These greens are too slow!
- I can't believe how cold it is today!
  - These greens are too fast!
- This is such a stupid game!
  - She has such good luck!
- I have such rotten luck!

Saying or thinking these things are a form of self-sabotage. It's your job to become AWARE (see Chapter Two!) of these thoughts and words, because they can so easily bring negative realities into your life.

> *You have to expect things of yourself before you can do them.*
>
> Michael Jordan

LIGHTEN UP!

We are not born with negative thoughts ... but we do give birth to them! Instead of doing that, we could be giving birth to thoughts like:

- My ball always gets good bounces!
- I love this hole!
- Isn't it a gorgeous day!
- Aren't these greens perfect!
- I love this game!

These words and thoughts will lighten your load and improve your attitude!

MY FAVORITE WORD: "OOPS"

The next time you play ... make a conscious choice to start the round with a positive, happy, "glass-half-full," "sky-mostly-sunny" attitude. Picture the ball going exactly where you want it go every time you step up to hit it. If the ball happens to go in a direction that was unintentional, just say, "Oops!" Take a completely non-judgmental, "oh, well" attitude to the shot. Choose that attitude. Then just let it go.

> *It wasn't a good shot. It wasn't a bad shot. It was just 'Oops!'*

MY ATTITUDE HERO

It's easier to change your own attitude for the better when you spend time with someone who knows how to change his or her own attitude for the better. Earlier, I asked you to think of someone you know personally who has a powerful positive attitude. You may want to start thinking of this person as your "attitude mentor."

Here's my attitude mentor: PGA Master Professional Gene Borek. I had the honor of working for Gene at Metropolis Country Club in White Plains, New York, for three years. Working for him was a truly life-affirming experience. He was the best boss I ever had! You knew what you'd get from Gene: a warm smile, a helping hand early in the morning and late at night, and always an amazing attitude. He never had anything bad to say about anyone, and he'd give you the shirt off his back with no expectation of receiving anything in return.

No matter how things were going for Gene, he always seemed okay with life – even when he was dealt some cards other people would have considered "bad breaks." He wasn't one to talk about himself in any negative way, and whenever you ran into him, he always wanted to know about how you were doing.

When Gene did talk about himself, he usually found a way to tell a great story from his long and successful career as a golf professional. His favorite story – one that I'm glad he never gets tired of telling — involves setting the course record (65) at the 1973 US Open at Oakmont.

When Gene was diagnosed with cancer years ago, his attitude remained as positive as ever. If you asked him how he was feeling, there was always a warm and believable smile behind his reply: "I'm doing fine." And he was! He wasn't interested in talking about his problems.

Gene is known among golf pros for his excellence as a teacher, his incredible talent as a player, and a heart big enough to share love with everyone he touches. He is the consummate gentleman. Anyone lucky enough to have been close to him in recent years knows that he is also the consummate human being. Gene is my "attitude hero!" When I want to know how I can upgrade my own attitude, I can always think of Gene and ask myself how he would respond to a situation.

So, Gene is my "attitude hero" – who's yours? You really should have a role model as you work to develop this part of your game – and your life.

> *People rarely succeed unless they have fun in what they are doing.*
>
> Dale Carnegie

To help you enhance a more positive Attitude refer to Appendix V - Attitude, for that Mind Power Stretching script.

Five: Attitude

Tommy's personal Garden back in time.

SIX

THE GARDEN

> *Kind hearts are the gardens,*
> *Kind thoughts are the roots,*
> *Kind words are the flowers,*
> *Kind deeds are the fruits.*
> *Take care of your garden, and keep out the weeds,*
> *Fill it with sunshine, kind words and kind deeds.*
>
> Henry Wadsworth Longfellow

The natural laws of the universe hold that what we think about is what we will receive in our lives. I have a special name for the place within where we can experience that law playing out for us: It's called the Garden.

This is the place inside of you, where you can always go for "soul food." It's here that you can directly experience the present-tense personal reality of your predominant thoughts – the thoughts that are manifesting in your life – the thoughts that are budding, blossoming and living inside of you.

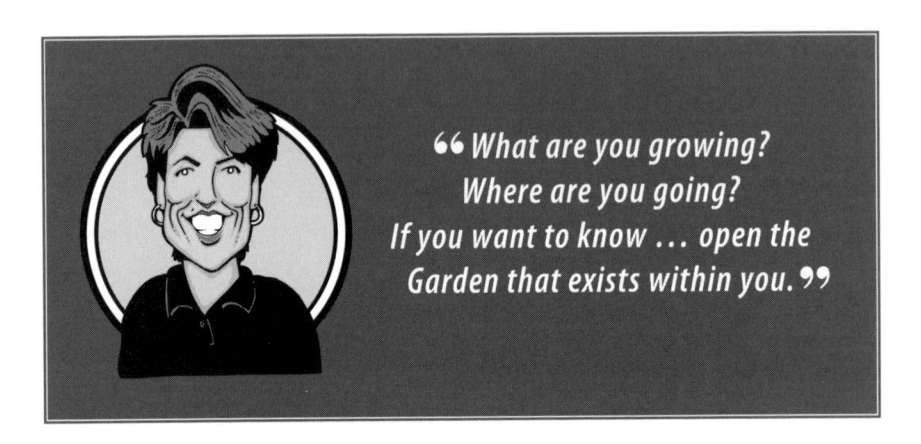

> *What are you growing?*
> *Where are you going?*
> *If you want to know ... open the Garden that exists within you.*

When I help people to improve their golf game with relaxation, guided imagery and mind triggers, I often use the image of a beautiful Garden. This image is a powerful one, because — as Longfellow knew — the Garden is the perfect metaphor for our own creative process, the process that is manifesting in our lives every day, whether we realize it or not.

Based on what you choose to think and visualize, your Garden can support vast stretches of weeds ... or it can support rich, abundant soil that blooms with thousands of colorful and fragrant flowers. Your inner gardener plants seeds or thoughts, which in turn produces growth — as the reality of your life.

At any given moment, your Garden is a reflection of who you are and what you are currently manifesting with your thoughts, feelings and desires. And you can enter it at any time.

You have two choices when it comes to managing your inner Garden (or any garden): a static approach or a dynamic approach.

Static Gardening:

1. You rarely or never enter the Garden, which means you allow weeds like fear, guilt, and anger to grow bigger and taller every day —overshadowing any possibility for new productive growth.

Dynamic Gardening:

2. You enter your inner Garden from time to time, clean out the weeds, and renew yourself. While you are there, you feed it and love the new growth you find.

There is no reason to be intimidated by the weeds in your Garden. Weeds pop up in every Garden. Fortunately, because this is a Garden of thought, it is much easier to tend than a physical Garden. You can pull a weed in this Garden simply by thinking and picturing for yourself, internally, *the thing you want to cultivate instead.*

By the same token, whenever you encounter a flower that you truly love, you can apply just a little of your own "miracle gro", — your thought-producing emotions —and then watch in wonder as your Garden becomes filled with colorful flowers, fresh herbs and blossoming new growth.

When you go inside yourself and encounter fear, you really can choose to cultivate love; when you encounter anger, you really can choose to cultivate happiness. You can also strengthen and expand every positive thought you encounter. Keep reading, and I'll show you how to do that.

Picture a beautiful Garden in your mind. It can be one you remember from childhood. Perhaps you can recall a class trip to a botanical Garden, or maybe you have a Garden now that is a safe and happy place for you to be. Whatever the best memory you have of a Garden is, I want you to enter that memory right now, and see yourself in that colorful and safe place

You really do have an internal Garden that corresponds to your favorite memory of a Garden. You can visit this internal Garden just by closing your eyes and thinking about the actual Garden from your memory. By closing your eyes and imagining that you are entering a special place, you are summoning your Garden into existence. This is a mystical place, a place deep inside of you. It's a safe place you can go to any time, a place you can make beautiful and vibrant, fertile and supportive of all your highest ambitions ... *if you choose to think thoughts that make the Garden more beautiful, as opposed to thoughts that make it more choked with weeds.*

- What is growing in your Garden right now?

- What are you feeding your Garden?

- Do you love and nurture the flowers in your Garden?

You can feed your Garden anything you choose, you know. You can create within your Garden any flower, any herb, and any crop you choose to manifest. All you have to do is start with one seed... one positive thought ... and then another.

It is entirely up to you.

> *The creation of a thousand forests is in one acorn.*
>
> Ralph Waldo Emerson

Let me tell you my favorite story about the Garden. Tommy is a Golf Professional at a country club; he plays and competes in many tournaments. One day, Tommy came to me for help.

Many people are surprised to learn that I coach golf professionals. The fact is, most pros are capable of hitting all the shots, yet still manage to get in their own way. Golf professionals know that the real obstacles are not a matter of external strategies and "tricks," but rather of internal awareness, communication with themselves, and sustained focus.

When I work with professionals, most of our time together is spent on the pre-shot routine and the act of visualizing the different shots. I help them create a movie they can play in their mind before each shot. I also teach them about mind triggers — images they see and thoughts they think which produce a good feeling and allow them to hit their best shot, consistently. All of this is in answer to the question I invariably hear from golf professionals:

If I know and understand so much about the game, how come I'm not playing better?

The answer to that question is almost always connected to the Garden they have grown for themselves.

When Tommy came to me, his goal was simple: He wanted to play golf with the same passion he had had as a young man. He wanted to play with joy and lightness in his heart. There was a secondary goal: he wanted to improve his score. But what he was really after was a feeling, an emotional state that connected to an exuberant style of playing the game that he had somehow lost sight of as a middle-aged man.

Now as a head golf professional who had been working at a country club for many years, who taught all day, who organized tournaments and ran the golf shop, Tommy found himself stuck. He had been doing this for a living for so long that he had he lost his childlike sense of "playing the game." Golf was his job. Tommy wanted to get back to having fun in golf, just like he used to!

I brought Tommy on a trip back in time, a trip that started with a journey to Tommy's personal Garden. We moved past the weeds – that is, the worries and concerns of his present day – and we went in search of some flowers. I asked him:

- What did his favorite corner of the Garden look like?
- What was growing there?
- What flowers did he like best?
- Where did he feel safest?

By visiting his internal Garden, his safest place, Tommy went into a state of deep relaxation very quickly, and together we started working backwards through the years.

What happened next was nothing short of astonishing.

In just a few minutes, this middle-aged golf professional was visualizing himself as a bright, energetic teenager doing what he loved to do, and could easily do all day long: playing golf.

Tommy told me about the vintage 1966 signs and the advertisements he encountered on the way to the local golf course. He was fifteen years old again. He recalled the sound of metal cleats as he walked through the parking lot toward the first tee. He envisioned the heavy leather Wilson bag he was carrying. He spoke of his original persimmon woods that were in the bag. *(That's back when fairway woods were actually made of wood.)*

He told me everything about the experience of golfing as a young man. As a boyish smile came to his face, he spoke of the details of the day as though he were actually back on that course in 1966. He told me everything he saw, everything he heard, everything he felt. He explained exactly what it felt like to play the game he loved, long before he became somebody who had to worry about mortgage payments and college tuition for his kids.

With his eyes closed, he told me, shot by exciting shot, about precisely what he was seeing, feeling and doing four decades ago. He was in a state of joy and pure love of the game. His smile continued as he spoke. He told me how happy he was, doing exactly what he loved to do—playing golf. His body language changed and softened.

I think the smile that played over his face as he took that journey back in time, was one of the most beautiful things I have ever seen.

A few weeks later, Tommy told me about a Senior event he had entered, and had done quite well in. "I was playing like a kid again," he told me. "It was great. I was playing from a totally different place! Once I stepped on the course, I left behind all of my outside challenges, and kept my thoughts in the present moment. It was wonderful!"

> *When I go into the garden with a spade, and dig a bed, I feel such an exhilaration and health that I discover that I have been defrauding myself all this time in letting others do for me what I should have done with my own hands.*
>
> Ralph Waldo Emerson

That's the power of your inner Garden! That's how easy it is to plant new dynamic growth that will move mountains out of your way.

Use your Garden to find the place where you can be the golfer – and the person – you were meant to be. Find the place where you feel good about yourself, and you will feel better about your golf game. Feed your Garden properly, and you'll begin to notice the results you want on the golf course. In the Appendix of this book, you will find a relaxation exercise that will help you to enter your Garden – just as Tommy entered his.

BILL

One spring day my student Bill and I were on the course working on the mental aspect of his golf game. At the fourth hole, we walked past a little meadow filled with fragrant lilies and wildflowers. A wonderful warm breeze wafted past us, and I thought to myself how very beautiful the scent of those flowers was.

When I glanced over at Bill, though, I noticed that his face was ashen, his body language tight, and his gaze suddenly narrow. Just a few minutes before, Bill and I had been talking and joking in a light-hearted way. Now, for some reason, his entire mood had changed.

I decided to raise his spirits.

"Wow, doesn't that smell wonderful?"

"What, I don't smell anything."

"The flowers… don't you smell those lilies?" I said. "Aren't they amazing?"

Bill's face remained a tight, grayish mask of self-protection. "I've always hated lilies," he said, his voice tense.

I couldn't believe my ears. "You've always hated lilies?" I asked. "They're some of my favorite flowers. They remind me of weddings and bar mitzvahs. When I was in college, I worked for a company that made videos of weddings and Bar Mitzvahs and other events. There were often beautiful lilies at those events, and I fell in love with the smell of that flower."

There was a little pause. Bill stared out at the sky for a moment.

"Lilies always remind me of funerals," he said finally.

I looked at him; I could tell he was troubled by something.

"I'm sorry to hear that," I said. "Was there one funeral that left a bigger connection with lilies than another for you?"

"Yes," Bill said. "There were lilies at my mother's funeral. I was only eleven years old."

There was another silence. "That must have been very hard for you, Bill."

"It was," he answered. "She loved flowers and kept them all over the house. When she died, I couldn't look at another flower for months. Now, every time I see a lily, or smell one, I think of her funeral."

I had touched on an association that was negatively affecting not only Bill's golf game, but quite possibly his entire life. He was now in his mid-forties; since he has been eleven, he had been going through the same negative process every time he encountered a lily, on the golf course or anywhere else. In his Garden, he had maintained a static, negative association with that particular experience. I wondered whether this was something that was holding him back in other areas of his life as well. On one level, the discussion was about Bill's reaction to lilies. On another, it might have been about long-standing issues related to his feelings for his mother, feelings that had been left unresolved for more than three decades.

I asked Bill whether he was willing to transform that negative association – simply by connecting it to something positive. In other words, I asked Bill if he wanted to use new thoughts as a kind of "miracle gro" to encourage new, dynamic growth in his Garden – growth that would help him to get out of his own way.

He seemed a little puzzled, but was interested in what I had to say.

HOW TO CHANGE THE SCENERY

Your inner Garden, like Bill's, is a part of your Baggage; it's what fills in your life story. You can alter it whenever you want. In Bill's case, he had strongly attached the experience of lilies with the emotion of his mother's funeral. But the simple fact that had connected a negative emotion to those flowers did not mean he was "locked into" that association for the rest of his life. At any point, he could "replant" the thought by attaching a happy event to it. There are two steps to this process. If there is something in your own past that feels similar to the almost-unconscious reaction that Bill had to seeing those lilies, you may want to implement these two steps yourself.

1. Become aware. Bill first had to become aware that he was connecting the look and smell of a lily to the emotions he had experienced at his mother's funeral.

2. Create a mind trigger. Once he was aware of the association, Bill could begin linking the sight and sound of a lily with another set of experiences. For instance: He could have associated the scent and appearance of lilies with the love he felt from his mother during time spent in a beautiful Garden with her when he was a child, or perhaps with the love he experienced when she placed flowers around the house. A process of guided relaxation and imagery can be helpful in starting this "rebirthing" process of one's mental associations – and beginning to plant a positive seed of thought in the Garden.

Doing what you've always done does not dictate what you'll always do!

> To help grow your own colorful Garden refer to Appendix VI - Garden, for that Mind Power Stretching script.

Six: The Garden

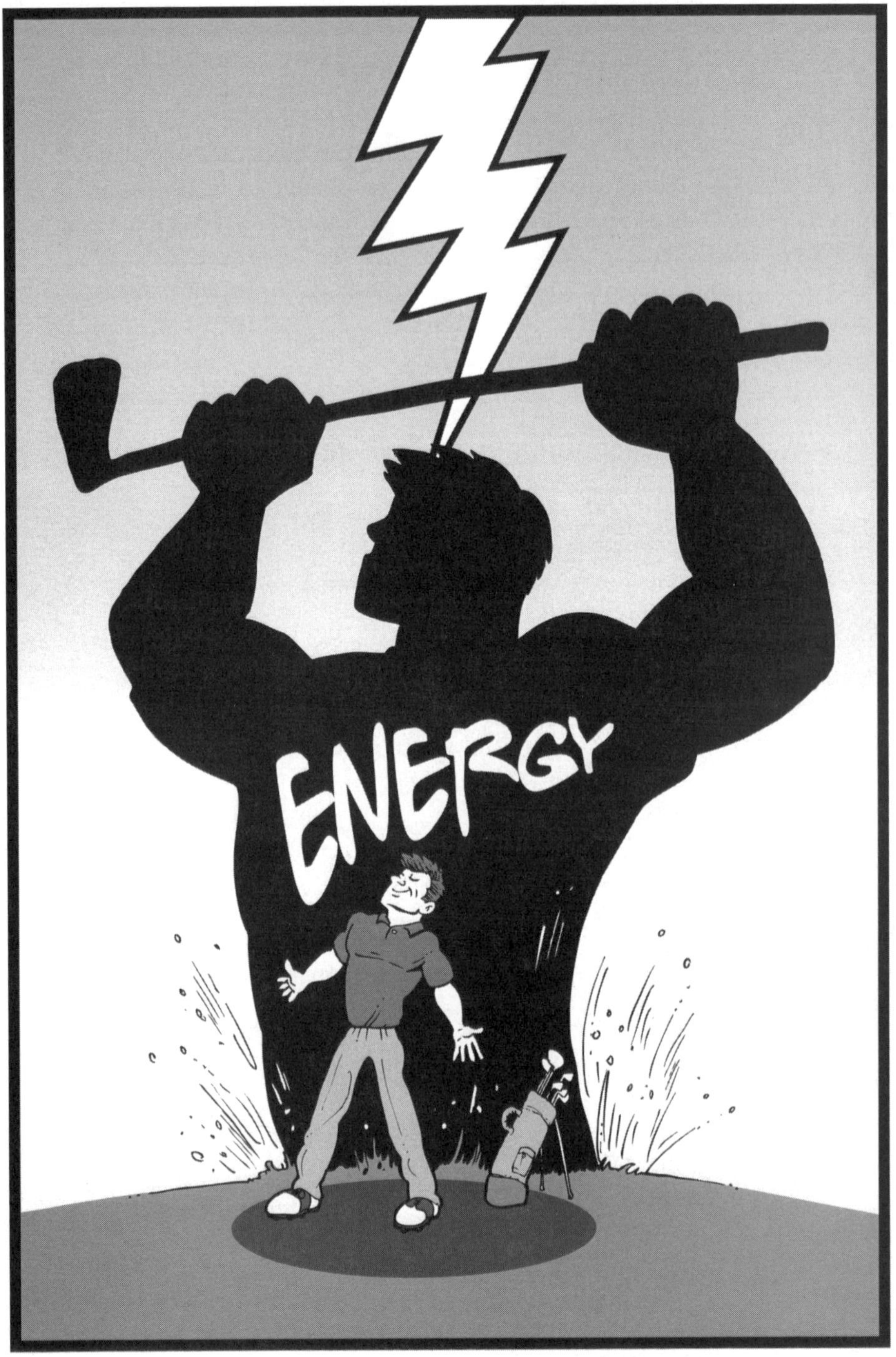
ENERGY

SEVEN

ENERGY

> *What this power is I cannot say.*
> *All I know is that it exists and becomes available only when a man is in that state of mind in which he knows exactly what he wants and is fully determined not to quit until he finds it.*
>
> Alexander Graham Bell

You can not *see* it, yet it gives you vision,
You can not *feel* it, yet it moves you,
You can not hear it, *yet* it whispers to you.

What is this mystical power? ... Energy!

Having first assimilated, and implemented, all that you have learned in the previous six chapters, you are now ready for the seventh and final lesson living within your Baggage.

Many people carry around with them, as part of their Baggage, the idea that something outside of themselves is responsible for how we feel. Summoning the Energy that will transform your emotions and improve your game in a dramatic way is entirely up to you. Accessing this Energy is not anyone else's responsibility or problem. As a matter of fact, the more you point the finger at others for your mishaps or challenges, the more this attitude *saps* Energy from you.

Let me be very clear about something. When I talk about *Energy*, with a capital E, I'm referring to something that has gone by many different names in many different cultures. The focus of this chapter is not so much about the calories you burn but rather a sustaining force that has, down the ages, been called many different things, by different people. Yet whatever we choose to call it, we are all talking about the same thing.

ENERGY EDUCATION

Back in the 1980s, when I first learned of this powerful force (a force I believe we are all endowed with), I was in massage school. The curriculum covered the basic Swedish massage technique, but it was another discipline, known as Amma Therapy, that really intrigued me. Amma, which is more than five thousand years old, means "push-pull" in Chinese. It is a remarkably powerful approach to massage; it taught me how to move energy through channels in the body. (I had learned similar principles, applied to my own body movements, when I studied Tai Chi.) Amma follows the same meridians or channels on the body as acupuncture, and focuses on balancing the body through the movement of energy. When you move blocked energy channels in accordance with Amma principles of massage, the body becomes dynamically balanced — and can literally heal itself.

PAY ATTENTION HERE!

The single most important lesson I learned in massage school was to be aware of, and not to take in, other people's negative energy.

How is it possible for the body to heal itself by moving energy around? How do you avoid taking in someone else's negative energy? Like anything else worth doing well, this kind of massage takes practice and patience. (Sounds a little like golf, doesn't it?) For me, a big part of that practice was learning how to understand my own energy.

Through deep breathing and various energy techniques, I discovered how to keep negative energy out — and retain my own powerful Energy, the life-giving Energy called, in Chinese traditions, Chi. Later in this chapter I'll show you how you can access your own Energy and move it around.

> *What's in a name? That which we call a rose by any other name would smell as sweet.*
>
> William Shakespeare

DIFFERENT NAMES YET THE SAME MEANING

Through the ages, Chi has been referred to as the Tao, Prana, the Spirit, and Cosmic Energy to name just a few. Chi Energy refers to the natural energy of the Universe that permeates everything and is all around us. It is our essential life force.

Whatever you choose to call this force – you will need to accept that there is something bigger and more powerful than your physical body, something that sustains you. Accept that you can call on that "something" at any time you want to improve your golf game, or to improve any other area of your life.

That "something" is Energy.

> *All the breaks you need in life wait within your imagination. Imagination is the workshop of your mind, capable of turning mind energy into accomplishment.*
>
> Dale Carnegie

IMAGINATION AND ENERGY

Some people get a little skeptical when I tell them that they really will need to accept that Energy, with a capital E, ultimately comes from a source larger than themselves. If you think back on the lessons that you've learned in the earlier chapters of this book, though, you'll realize that much of what you've been learning to do has been simply using your imagination to help you "get out of your own way." Everything you've learned in the pages preceding this chapter have been leading up to what you're about to learn, namely how to tap into the same Energy that has been guiding you through all the lessons of your life, so you can focus it on a specific goal: Improving your golf game. Tapping into the Energy that guides and nourishes us all is, in the final analysis, the only way to accomplish anything worth accomplishing. And that definitely includes bringing your golf game up to another level.

We are all Energy!

This Energy is the power that enables us to think, move, breathe, and live. It is the power that makes gravity and electricity possible. It is the link between our perception of the inner and outer worlds. We can't see it … but we do know for certain that it exists!

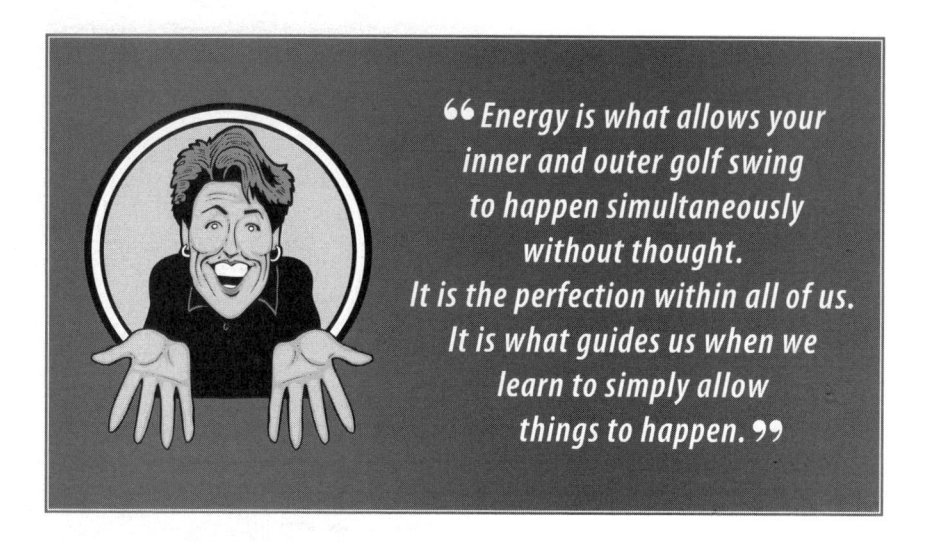

> **❝ Energy is what allows your inner and outer golf swing to happen simultaneously without thought. It is the perfection within all of us. It is what guides us when we learn to simply allow things to happen. ❞**

Energy is what makes breathing possible.

It creates movement and thought.

It's the oxygen in our lungs, and the blood in our veins.

It lives in us, through us and completes us.

> You cannot *see* it, yet it gives you vision.
>
> You cannot *feel* it, yet it moves you.
>
> You cannot *hear* it, yet it whispers to you.
>
> You cannot *smell* or taste it, yet it feeds your desires.

ENERGY IS THE COMPLETENESS OF ALL YOUR SENSES… IT IS YOUR SIXTH SENSE!

It is up to you to let the Energy sink in and permeate your soul. It is up to you to accept this great gift and let it start to work through you.

WHAT YOU ARE THINKING = HOW YOU ARE FEELING

- What are you thinking right now?
- How are you feeling right now?
- Are you feeling good?

Take a moment and reflect on these questions. *They are very important.*

Remember how we explored the essential role your emotions play in lowering your golf score? Your feelings are a reflection of your thoughts, and **your thoughts are Energy.**

As you read these words, I'm asking you to closely consider your actual, present-tense thoughts and your actual, present-tense emotional state. I'm asking you to do that right now, because I want you to notice, and learn to use to your advantage, an important Energy Principle. It is this.

Right now, at this moment:

You are either being brought up to a higher level that will allow you to dynamically perform, inside and out, at an optimum level ….

OR

You are being pulled down to a level that obstructs Energy, a level that statically diminishes optimum performance.

HEADS OR TAILS … YOU CHOOSE!

Unlike the 50/50 chance you have when flipping a coin, your choices determine 100% of this outcome. So: Which direction is it going to be? To know, you must pay close attention to your own thoughts and feelings.

Your Energy is like a river. You are either paddling with the current or paddling against it. The only reliable way to tell whether you are paddling with the current or paddling against it is to ask yourself these questions:

- *What am I thinking right now?*
- *How am I feeling right now?*
- *Am I feeling good or bad?*

The ability to ask yourself these simple questions is what makes the difference between a life thrown away and a life well lived.

ARE YOU WILLING AND OPEN?

If you are willing to ask yourself these questions as you make your way through the day, and as you connect with your golf game ….

… if you are willing to stop and give your full attention and then answer them honestly …

… if you are willing to overcome the strong instinct to "come back to them later" ….

… then congratulations. You have begun the process of taking personal responsibility for what you are actually feeding into your system. You have begun the process of managing your internal Energy.

There is an art to understanding your own thoughts and feelings, and developing a sense of whether they are giving you pleasure, raising you up, and allowing you to access more Energy … or drawing you down. There is an art to overcoming, with conscious effort, thoughts and feelings that are keeping you from accessing the Energy that is your birthright.

Mastering that art is the work of a lifetime.

Practicing that art is the gift you have been given right now!

Doing this is not your boss's job. It is not your mother's job. It is not your father's job. It is not your spouse or ex-spouse's job. In fact, it is no one's *job* at all. It should never feel like a job or something you resent doing. It should be a joy to realize that you can call Energy into your life whenever you need it.

When you learn to "take your own temperature" by paying attention to your own thoughts and feelings ... when you can notice the direction in which your thoughts and feelings are sending you ... when you can do that *effortlessly*, you're doing it right.

And *the only person who can possibly do this is you.*

WHAT YOU GIVE OUT IS WHAT YOU GET BACK

When you are constantly waiting for a group in front of you, what happens? Do you think to yourself, "What a beautiful day! I could play all day ... I'm really swinging well today. I feel good ... I am so grateful to be here doing this."

Let's call that kind of thinking Approach A.

Or, alternatively, do you think to yourself, "Look at them – chatting and joking — wasting everyone's time, taking forever. I can't believe we're stuck behind these people. What a lost cause this day turned out to be – I wanted to relax, but I can't possibly be expected to relax with these slowpokes in front of me all morning."

Let's call that kind of thinking Approach B.

> **❝ *Thinking the first category of thoughts, the thoughts about how grateful you are to be out golfing, the thoughts about how lucky you are to be doing something you love, will bring similar thoughts into your mind, more gratitude, and more access to the Energy that will help you improve.* ❞**

On the other hand, thinking the second kind of thoughts, the thoughts about how you are "wasting" your morning waiting for somebody else, will attract more of those thoughts into your mind, and reduce your access to the Energy that could have helped you to improve.

What you give out is what you get back. That means what you get back is entirely up to you.

So. Are you going in the direction you want to go with your thoughts? What do you want to think, right now? How would thoughts of gratitude and love make you feel, right now?

"I CAN'T STAND IT, IT'S SO SLOW!"

After a Keynote presentation I gave a few years ago, a woman asked me a great question about something that has happened to almost everyone at some time on the course. She was a fairly fast player and asked me how she should handle slow play. She said she can feel her blood pressure rise when she has to play with a slow player. She said it's usually a member/guest or a tournament, so it is not her choice to pair up with them.

So I posed this very important question to her, and I want you to think about it as well.

"What are your choices?"

I mean let's be honest and keep it simple. She didn't understand the question and said, "I don't have a choice, that's why I get so mad!" So before she got too irritated, I told her she needed to send out some love!

She looked at me sideways *(more like I had two heads)* and said, "Excuse me?" I explained to her about the law of attraction and the power of gratitude. What you give out, you get back. So you need to choose what it is you want, and remember that what you send out you get back. You can:

A) Send some love! While you're waiting for others to play their game (that's the part that is out of your control), look around at the beautiful scenery, listen to the birds and the leaves rustling in the wind, enjoy the fresh sunshine and really appreciate where you are. Patiently wait for her to play her game until it is your turn to hit.

OR

B) Stomp around in irritation, huff and puff waiting for her to "play her game" while she's enjoying her game, obviously not bothered by you. At the same time you ruin your game with a negative attitude that depletes all your focus and positive energy.

What are your choices? Play the game and enjoy whatever the day has dealt you or walk off the course and leave. BUT… is that really what you want? I don't think so. Whenever you are in a quandary, always ask yourself the question, "what are my choices?" Just ask yourself which one is going to make you stronger, increase your mind power and energize you. The answer will appear as clear as a blue sky.

THE ART OF STEPPING ASIDE

Learn to notice your thoughts and emotions. Learn to step gently aside from them if they don't support you. Invest in your power to create thoughts and emotions to summon Energy that will sustain and excite you on the golf course … and everywhere else you go.

Make a personal commitment to step aside from Approach B thinking whenever you notice it. It takes practice, but you can learn to do it … if you *notice* what you are thinking and feeling, and if you practice stepping aside.

If you have ever gotten advice similar to this before, and are resistant right now, I have a question for you. When you rejected that advice …. what were you thinking? Was it something like this?

"I know. I'm not supposed to think negative. Believe me I've tried. I just can't do it.

I get mad at things. That's who I am!"

What would you have to say to yourself to turn this into a thought that STEPS GENTLY ASIDE from Approach B? Maybe it would sound like this:

"As time passes, I understand this more completely and I do get better at this. I choose to think about whatever I want. I've built

up a lot of resilience, which means I'm good at practicing. I can do this. I can find things I like about golf. I love golf!"

EASY WAYS TO DO THIS

Keep a positive focus on the golf course by ....

… noticing the beauty of the nature that surrounds you as you play. (It really is quite beautiful. Notice that.)

… listening to positive music before you start the game. (You can then "hear" your favorite music in your head which will lift you up and help you stay focused.)

…. thinking of and picturing someone you love without reservation, and who loves you without reservation. (Even better; hang a picture of this person on your golf bag.)

… thinking of and picturing a favorite pet. (This is an *incredibly* effective technique. I have plenty of clients who keep photos of their dog or cat nearby whenever they play golf. You should know that, in order to take advantage of the powerful positive feelings that people have about their pets, I always ask students I coach if they have a pet and what their name is. Then, at a key point in my sessions with them, I can encourage them to visualize positive memories that involve a pet. It works!)

What brings you joy changes your thoughts and feelings to joyful ones, and brings you Energy. Find a way to visualize that which brings you joy!

With practice, you will develop a powerful new belief *(Chapter One)* about yourself:

"I'm the kind of person who easily summons joyous Energy into my life."

PHYSICALLY SUMMONING ENERGY

The healing, reviving force of Energy is yours whenever you wish. It is simpler to access than you might think. *This Energy will improve your golf game, or anything else that needs improving in your life: any activity, any relationship, any response to illness – anything!*

First, realize that the true secret to acquiring your dynamic Energy lives in your breathing.

Breathing in and out through the nose is the best way for the body to process Energy effectively. More importantly when we breathe out through the nose rather than the mouth we retain a greater amount of Energy.

HOW IT WORKS

Basically, when we inhale, we are bringing in fresh oxygen and Energy. When we exhale through the mouth, we are expelling carbon dioxide, which contains all the toxins and poisons that have built up within the lungs. However, we are also releasing Energy from the body.

If you continue to expel the Energy, you never give it a chance to build up for maximum effectiveness. By exhaling through the mouth, you allow the Energy to disperse back into the world.

THE CLOSED CIRCUIT

Exhaling through the nose, rather than the mouth, transfers the Energy into a spot located about three fingers below your navel. With each breath we take in, more Energy enters the body and circles down to this spot below your navel, growing stronger and stronger.

(This spot, known as tan tien in Asian healing, is our core or center. It is where all power originates and moves from. It is the balancing point of the yin and yang.)

Energy is a subtle, invisible force that requires patience and practice to summon. When your mind and body are working together and you are breathing properly, a tremendous amount of Energy can flow through you. The key is not to force it, but rather to slow down, relax, and breathe through your nose.

Below, you'll find other tools to help you draw more Energy into your life. Realize at any time a) it if it ever feels like a chore, it won't work, and b) it will only work if you are *willing to use it to turn what you are thinking and feeling in the dynamic direction of joy.*

ENERGY LESSONS

The first step is simple: become aware of the capacity of your lungs.

To start, imagine the lungs are two balloons inside the chest. As you breathe normally, the top third of these balloons is filled and emptied. All day, every day, the top third of your lungs are typically all that is being used to keep you alive — while the bottom two thirds remain unused.

Dynamic conscious breathing teaches you how to breathe from the bottom of the lungs up, expanding them to their full capacity. With expanded use of your lungs, the intake of oxygen is increased dramatically and more oxygen-rich blood circulates within the body. Here are three Energy enhancing, breathing lessons.

1) LUNG CAPACITY ENHANCER

1. Exhale completely, and breathe in slowly through the nose.

2. Imagine filling the balloons up from the bottom, relaxing the ribcage and stomach muscles. Concentrate on maximizing the expansion of the lungs.

3. Come to a full stop, then open your mouth and inhale some more.

4. Top off your lungs with a quick intake of breath. Even if you don't think you can.

5. Hold your breath for a moment and then (from your nose) exhale completely, forcing out as much air as possible by contracting the muscles of the ribcage and stomach.

6. Repeat two more times with your eyes closed. Become aware of how the balloons fill and expand in size each time. Notice if there are any changes in your chest or elsewhere in your body.

Good Job!

2) THE BREATH OF JOY

You can do this exercise either seated or standing.

1. Right now, think of someone, something or someplace you love.

2. Experience the joy that accompanies thinking about that person, pet, or place.

3. With your mouth closed, take a deep breath in through your nose. As you inhale, feel the breath extending down all the way to the base of your spinal column.

4. Picture the person, pet, place. (Keep your mouth closed!)

5. Release the breath slowly through your nose.

6. Now repeat it with your eyes closed. (Yes, you can do this on the golf course. It only takes a few seconds.)

This is your first step to tapping into dyanmic Energy and will soon become a habit! Reinforce that habit. When you're ready to plunge deeper, go to the next lesson.

> *Love, compassion, kindness and wonder are associated with deep, comfortable breathing and an open receptive feeling throughout the entire body.*
>
> The Tao of Natural Breathing by Dennis Lewis.

3) THE SPHERE OF ENERGY

This is a powerful way to enhance what you want (your goals) by means of pure dynamic Energy. It connects physical movement and mental concentration into a powerful energy force. It is simple and extremely effective. Let's do it!

1. Think of your goal (or anything you want in life.) Breathe deeply in… and then out.

2. Rub your hands quickly together and create warmth and friction. Keep going! Feel the Energy building… Really feel your hands getting warmer and warmer!

3. After at least 10-15 seconds, separate your hands as though you were holding a basketball.

4. Feel the Sphere of Energy pulsating between your hands.

5. Think about your goal now and state your desire out loud or quietly to yourself.

6. Say, "Upon this sphere of energy, I want _____" (fill in the blank), while at the same time… look out to the universe, and throw your hands (the sphere of Energy) out. Let it go.

7. Now be patient and let that Energy you just released, come back to you!

YOU ARE A POWER SOURCE

Moving from static ("not much going on") to dynamic ("something's happening here") Energy occurs when you consciously become aware of your own body and the incredible potential stored within it. Becoming aware of the air you breathe is a great way to reach that feeling. When you expand your breathing ability … you increase and stretch your Energy potential.

BECOME AWARE OF YOUR BREATHING

At any time of the day, anywhere you are, stop and notice your breathing. Take a deeper breath. No matter what you are doing, breathe. Make conscious, dynamic breathing a regular part of your life.

Like the other six lessons in your Baggage, Energy is an invisible force that requires patience. When your mind and body are integrated, a tremendous amount of Energy is able to flow through you. The key is not to force it, but instead simply to slow down, relax and breathe. And whenever you can (for instance, tonight as you are going to sleep), ask yourself:

- Am I going in the direction I want to go with my thoughts?
- What do I *want* to think, right now?
- How would thoughts of gratitude and love make me feel, right now?

GOOSE BUMPS

Have you ever noticed goose bumps appear on your arm as you listen to a great story, or agreeing with what someone just told to you? As you move into a place of enlightened energy, and all that you've been asking for is being delivered to you, those goose bumps will show up more and more. Realize it is then that you are in vibrational harmony with the universe, within yourself, and *Your Inner Swing*!

To help you create a new Energy force in golf and life refer to Appendix VII - Energy, for that Mind Power Stretching script.

EPILOGUE

Most readers don't get this far in a book of this nature, so congratulations for getting here. Great job! It takes patience and understanding to change things that have been there for a long time. Because you've read the previous chapters, you now realize the only way for things to change, is for you to change them.

I believe to "get" this kind of book to work for you, you will probably want to read again the parts that got you enthusiastic or excited. This is the best way to gain more insight into the inner workings of you and your life story — otherwise known Baggage.

THE INNER ALWAYS FEEDS THE OUTER

So here is the inner question I asked at the onset of this book. Let me ask you again. How long can you go without inner food, water or air to nourish you from the inside out?

You can't! It's the same with your thoughts.

Your inner thoughts feed your outer world. Think of your thoughts, feelings and emotions as the "food, water, and air" you are using internally to create that which you manifest in the outside world. Your combined internal Energy — within your Baggage— is what provides the synergy in your world. It's what makes things come together. It's what makes the "whole you" greater than the sum of your parts.

Once you learn to master your thoughts and use your emotions, you will begin to take dynamic control of the direction of your Baggage .. and of ultimately *Your Inner Swing* … in golf… and of your life!

How are you breathing, right now? Deep or shallow?

YOUR ALADDIN'S LAMP

Wouldn't it be great if we all had an Aladdin's Lamp to wish things into being? Wouldn't it be great if you could pick up the lamp, rub it back and forth a couple of times, and be greeted by a Genie always saying the same thing, "Your wish is my command"?

If you take control of your thoughts and use your emotion as a tool to support and sustain yourself ... your wish IS YOUR command! The Law of Attraction states that what you think about is what you will bring about. Your thoughts bring more like thoughts to you. It's the Energy of your thoughts moving in various directions that determines the Energy, the experience, and the results you get back.

Do you believe it is now possible to have your very own Aladdin's lamp? I am going to answer that for you with a "YES"!

PUSH YOUR FAITH BUTTON

Your ultimate faith comes from within. It is this inner faith that gives you the ability to go inside and make all the changes you need. This faith is all you need to build the Inner Swing that is right for you.

Faith to **Believe** in yourself.

Faith to be **Aware** of what you want.

Faith to be **Grateful** for everything in your world.

Faith to create and complete your **Goals**.

Faith in your **Attitude** to move you in the right direction.

Faith in your inner **Garden** to grow wonderful and beautiful things.

And the **Energy** to have faith in everything you do.

What are you going to do right now to use these seven lessons in golf and life to move yourself dynamically forward?

APPENDIX

Here you'll find additional material for expanding and reprogramming *your inner swing*. Mind Power Stretching (MPS), otherwise known as hypnosis, allows you to change your thoughts, ideas and perceptions on a subconscious level. Since your Baggage is filled with your life story, or more likely your perception of that story, it can be changed. Here is the place to make even more wonderful changes to enhance your golf… and life.

Hypnosis is a state of mind in which the conscious mind or critical factor is bypassed, and the subconscious mind non-critically accepts suggestions for change. Common hypnosis treatments that you may be aware of are used to quit smoking, lose weight and even to overcome the fear of flying, (which is pretty important if you want to play golf around the world). And although I can work with anyone using my hypnotherapy training, this is primarily for the golfer's mental performance improvement.

The pages that follow are about helping your game improve on a subconscious level. These are scripts that I've created based on the seven chapters. There's no doubt that what you've read about in each chapter will help you tremendously. And, the journey you are about to take is like no other.

"Going inside" (as my Hypnotherapy teacher would say) and opening your mind subconsciously will move you up the performance platform. All of your thoughts, feelings and memories are housed in your subconscious mind. When you "go inside" and quiet your mind, you clean out the cobwebs creating clarity and room to breathe deeply.

UNDERSTANDING MEANS NOTHING TO FEAR

Each script consists of an induction, suggestion and awakening. The induction guides you to a beautiful place in nature which relaxes your conscious thinking mind, and allows your subconscious mind to listen. Suggestions are then introduced to your subconscious mind for acceptable change. I say acceptable because you control what you will let in. Suggestions are only ideas for you to accept or deny. The third part is the awakening and means just what the word implies. This is a gentle nudge back into full consciousness to the place you started your journey. Even if you happen to fall asleep during the session (if you are listening rather than reading), your subconscious hears everything... it always does. (FYI – that's why you should never go to sleep with the TV on, you never know what the subconscious hears.)

This is the easiest stretch you've ever done!

Stretch – *(def.) to make full use of abilities or intellect; to extend something excessively so that the shape is permanently altered.*

To stretch something is to expand something greatly for a lasting change. Mind Power Stretching (MPS) is expanding your subconscious thoughts to create lasting change! This is a powerful proven method for improving your golf game – and your life.

Practice Session

Unlike physical stretching, mind power stretching only involves your imagination... cool huh? To change your thoughts, you must get all of your senses involved.

Let's do a warm-up right now, (like hitting balls at the range before going out to play).

First step: Picture a really good food, a food that you like... perhaps even your FAVORITE food. If you can't think of one, try a slice of hot, steamy, cheesy pizza.

See it in your mind. Take in all the colors and textures.

Now **smell** the wonderful aroma wandering up towards your nose.

Breathe in deeply through your nose now and take in all the smells.

Getting ready to taste it now.

You may even have started to salivate.

Now pick up the fork or the pizza with your hands.

Feel the weight and texture in your hands as you lift it towards your mouth.

Bringing the food towards your mouth now... notice any sensations starting to happen?

Now **taste** it, enjoy the flavor, chewing slowly savoring each and every bite completely.

To finish the process **swallow** it, enjoying the entire experience to the fullest!

(Make a mental note of what you crave in the next 24 hours... it might surprise you!)

*Using your **senses** REALLY WORKS when it comes to changing your thinking and belief patterns. This gives you an idea of what we'll be doing throughout the appendix exercises.*

For each MPS piece I suggest any of the following:

1. Read the following material to yourself. Some of information will get past your conscious mind and allow your subconscious to listen. Then sit quietly and let what you've read sink in for fifteen minutes or so.

2. (More effective) Record the material or have someone read it to you so you can listen with your eyes closed. Your mind listens and absorbs better when your eyes are closed.

3. (Most effective) - Use a professionally made version from www.YourInnerSwing.com. Just click on **Book Downloads** and enter the password **golfmindpower4me** for the download.

APPENDIX I - BELIEFS

Here are **Belief** affirmations that are based on what you learned in that chapter.

Say these to yourself morning and night. Write them down and place them somewhere for daily viewing, like a bathroom mirror, refrigerator or nightstand. Read them often, as repetition is the key to your development. *(These are also placed in the suggestion segment.)*

- I believe my inner mind is strong and resilient.

- I believe my golf game is getting better and better.

- My beliefs are my own and I believe only what I want to believe.

- I believe I can stretch my inner mind to help me in every way.

- I believe in my ability to improve on and off the golf course.

- My beliefs guide me to positive outcomes in golf and life.

- I use beliefs *that do not support me as insight for supporting beliefs that do!*

Now create your own Belief affirmations:

_____

_____

What follows will create a total relaxation of body and mind. Tension is released as the conscious mind drifts in and out. It's common that mental images arise of forgotten events held in the subconscious, the computer-like mind that houses all thoughts and memories from the past.

> *Find a quiet place where you won't be disturbed for 15-20 minutes. Turn off the phones and any disturbances. Recline or lie flat with your arms parallel to your body and feet separated.*

Make yourself comfortable. Read slowly taking an occasional pause between paragraphs.

Begin by closing your eyes and taking a deep breath in through your nose. Hold it for the count of three and exhale from your nose slowly. Relax now. Take another deep breath in, and as you slowly exhale, feel a wave of relaxation move from the top of your head all the way down your body to the tips of your toes, relaxing you even deeper. Allow yourself to take a journey inside.

Imagine with me that you're strolling along on a beautiful, tropical island. It's a warm, sunny afternoon; the sky is a pretty shade of blue and the sea is sparkling with effervescence. The waves are dancing and splashing up to the shore and the white sand is warm beneath your bare feet.

And as you're slowly walking along on the soft white sand, you can feel the soft grains between your toes, and you're taking in the beautiful view, the deep blue ocean, the lovely white sand and the clearest blue sky.

There is no one else in sight, there's just the sound of birds singing some place in the distance. It's so calm here, and so peaceful. This is your paradise. Your own, very special, very private place, where you can come, and relax, at anytime you wish. Always remember that. You can come here any time that you want to – all with the power of your own inner mind – all you need to do is relax – and let go.

Take a deep breath in ... and with each following breath, allow yourself to become more and more deeply relaxed. Just let your eyes roll back in your head as your arms and legs become heavier and heavier.

You are now becoming deeply, deeply relaxed... and the suggestions that you will hear will have an immediate effect on your subconscious mind - you will hear every word that I speak - even though you may find your mind wandering away at times - right now - nothing else matters - except for this wonderful feeling of relaxation that you are experiencing.

At this moment it's as though you haven't a care in the world - nobody wants anything - nobody needs anything - there is absolutely nothing at all for you to do except relax, unwind and let go - just enjoy the feelings that are being generated within you.

And I wonder if you can now imagine finding a comfortable place to sit, on the sand. Everything is so calm – and so peaceful.

And you're just sitting there; listening to the sound of the powerful waves breaking against the shore ... you may notice a gentle breeze against your skin, and the radiant sun, so warm, against your body... you can feel the light from the sun radiating around your body... warming you gently, all over.

Now as you look down the shoreline you notice a boat anchored up on the shore. This is your boat... it's waiting just for you. It can be any size boat you wish. It may be a small row boat or a large sail boat. Anything you want it to be... this is your boat.

In a moment I want you to see yourself walk over to this boat. In a moment you will have the opportunity to free your mind of any Self-Limiting beliefs... that may have been holding you back from your true unlimited potential in your golf game... as well as in your life.

Take a deep breath in, and as you let it out, let your body completely relax and go deeper. Now imagine yourself walking along the warm white beach and towards the waters edge where the boat is anchored. When you arrive at the boat you may notice a feeling stirring inside of you. These are the beliefs you no longer need or want to carry around with you.

Maybe at one time those beliefs served and helped you. They may have even helped you get where you are right now. You NOW realize there may be negative Beliefs that you have been carrying around for a very long time... you NOW realize you no longer need them. ... So go ahead and toss them on to the boat now. You may want to imagine opening your mind to release them and throw them on the boat. I will stop talking for a short time... to allow you to do that now.

(Pause for 30-60 seconds)

Good... you are concentrating perfectly at letting go of past beliefs. Release any lasting old beliefs now... and in a moment we will send the boat far, far away. I want you to now imagine the boat's anchor is being lifted. The ocean's current is starting to take the boat out to sea. All that you have released is being taken far, far out to sea... the boat is getting smaller and smaller as it gets farther and farther away. Until it is so far away that it is out of your sight... and now completely out of your mind.

Your subconscious mind is ready to listen and move forward with new beliefs that will help you and move you in the direction of positive thinking. Now that you have released your old beliefs that were part of your old Baggage, the following affirmations will help you move in a more positive direction. Repeat these in your mind after me:

- *I believe my inner mind is strong and resilient.*

- *I believe my golf game is getting better and better.*

- *My beliefs are my own and I believe only what I want to believe.*

- *I believe I can stretch my inner mind to help me in every way.*

- *I believe in my ability to improve on and off the golf course.*

- *My beliefs guide me to positive outcomes in golf and life.*

- *I use beliefs that do not support me as insight for supporting beliefs that do!*

Insert your own affirmations or repeat from the previous page.

_____

_____

_____

Good - now you may decide to come back if you feel that you've missed something - and continue to dispose of any unwanted thoughts or feelings or emotions ... when you're ready you can now begin to work on your new beliefs - one thought at a time. You work on new beliefs one thought at a time. Your new beliefs get stronger and stronger every day.

And you start by doing good things for yourself - just simple things at first - like treating yourself to something special— looking into the mirror and smiling and telling yourself that you love who you are. You identify all the nice things about your personality - what qualities would your best friend say you have?

And you know more than you think you know - you trust your subconscious mind, you love and respect yourself - you do good things for yourself - and you feel really good about yourself - this makes others feel good about you.

You have now moved into a new and powerful state of clear thoughts and emotions. You know your emotions change when your thoughts change. In order to change anything ... you must first become aware of negative self-limiting beliefs... and change your thoughts into positive empowering beliefs. From this moment on, you now choose clear and positive thoughts. These thoughts bring you a high frequency of good and loving emotional Energy. You have chosen this new way of thinking by releasing the old beliefs that no longer serve you.

These suggestions are firmly embedded in your subconscious mind... They become stronger and stronger day by day.

Now - when you're ready - I'm going to count from one to five. At the count of five you'll be wide awake feeling fully rested, refreshed and energized.

Number One – noticing the positive mind power now within you… as your body and mind have been relaxed, cleansed and revitalized.

*Number Two – sensing new **Beliefs**, emotions and energy that has expanded inside of you.*

Number three – noticing the material beneath you… Your breathing is becoming more regular, and you are coming slowly back to the place you started.

Number four – feeling fantastic in every way… and on the next number you will be alert, recharged and refreshed with energy.

Number five – take a deep breath in, stretch your arms and open your eyes when you're ready.

Welcome Back!

APPENDIX II - AWARENESS

Affirmations:

Here are some **Awareness** affirmations that are based on what you learned in that chapter.

Say these to yourself morning and night. Write them down and place them somewhere for daily viewing, like a bathroom mirror, refrigerator or nightstand. Read them often as repetition is the key to your development.

- I am now aware of stretching my inner mind for my ultimate good.
- My awareness moves me beyond negative thoughts and into positive ones.
- I am aware that my golf improves when my thoughts improve.
- I am now aware of thoughts, feelings and emotions that improve my life completely.
- I control my inner thoughts by becoming aware of them.
- I am aware of thoughts that consistently enhance my golf game.
- I am now aware of new and wonderful thoughts that surround and support me.

Create your own Awareness affirmations:

_____

_____

_____

> *Find a quiet place where you won't be disturbed for 15-20 minutes. Turn off the phones and any disturbances. Recline or lie flat with your arms parallel to your body and feet separated. Make yourself comfortable. Read slowly taking an occasional pause between paragraphs.*

(Record the following or download it at www.yourinnerswing.com)

Begin by closing your eyes and taking a deep breath in, hold it for the mental count of three and exhale slowly, relax now. Take another deep breath in, and as you slowly exhale feel a wave of relaxation move from the top of your head all the way down your body to the tips of your toes, relaxing even deeper.

As you relax even more deeply I want you to picture this scene in your mind. It's a lovely warm summer's day and you are walking through a shady wooded area - and although it's shady here, the air is warm and the sun streams through the trees, lighting up patches of grass and flowers here and there.

Listen to the birds singing in the trees, as you walk barefoot on the soft green grass... and notice how good it feels to your toes, as you stroll along. Just ahead of you is a lovely little pond.

Beside the pond, on a grassy mound there is a wonderful large tree brimming with life and full-size green leaves. You wander over and sit down on the grass beside the pond. It is crystal clear, reflecting every light and shadow... it reflects the clear blue of the sky, little skittering clouds, the leaves on the tree, and your own face.

Just as you are enjoying these lovely reflections, a sudden gust of wind comes along, and before you know it, the surface of the pond has been covered with the leaves that have blown from the tree. All of the reflections are gone... obscured by the leaves.

You watch the leaves floating on the surface... and in a few minutes you realize that they are moving, gently propelled by the current in the pond.

Some of them seem to be just swirling slowly, aimlessly about... but some of them have begun to drift to the edge of the pond, coming to rest along the edges of the bank, drifting gently and purposefully, towards the end of the pond. And soon, once more, you begin to see the reflections of the sky, and the tree, and your own face.

And as you rest here, you can become aware of the magical qualities of this lovely little pond, actually flowing into your feet and into your legs and body and arms and head. You feel yourself drifting further and further into a quiet sense of peacefulness. You are drifting, deeper and deeper down.

And as your body relaxes, so does your mind... and the magic flows into your mind, relaxing, cleansing and clearing your mind of all clutter and unnecessary thoughts that you now become aware of. Washing away any negative thoughts, and leaving room for healthy, more positive thoughts and feelings.

In a moment you will hear some new, positive, healthy thoughts, that you become more aware of day by day. Just let your mind receive... and act upon the messages you are about to hear.

Your subconscious mind is ready to listen and move you up to a higher frequency on your Emotional Energy Ladder™. Your awareness carries thoughts, feelings and emotions that support you.

Now that you are becoming more and more aware of your thoughts... day by day... the following affirmations will help you move in a more positive direction to new optimistic thoughts. Repeat these in your mind after me:

- *I am now aware of stretching my inner mind for my ultimate good.*

- *My awareness moves me beyond negative thoughts and into positive ones.*

- *I am aware that my golf improves when my thoughts improve.*

- *I am now aware of thoughts, feelings and emotions that improve my life completely.*

- *I control my inner thoughts by becoming aware of them.*

- *I am aware of thoughts that consistently enhance my golf game.*

- *I am now aware of new and wonderful thoughts that surround and support me.*

Insert your own affirmations or repeat the above.

_____

_____

_____

Good - now you may decide to come back if you feel that you've missed something - and continue to dispose of any unwanted thoughts that do not make you feel good ... when you're ready... you can now begin your new inner awareness... You have the ability to move up your own emotional ladder... one thought at a time, one step at a time. You are becoming aware ...one thought at a time. This new awareness gets stronger every day in every way.

And you start by noticing things around you that have been there all along - just simple things at first - like colorful flowers and blossoming trees, cute little animals scampering around, and the awareness of a baby giggling and laughing that makes you stop and smile. Take time to reflect on things you may not have been aware of. This new you can look in the mirror and smile... simply aware that you love who you are.

And you know more than you think you know - you trust your subconscious mind... you love and respect yourself - you do good things for yourself - and you feel really good about who you are - this makes others feel good about you... and want to be around you. You are aware of this wonderful change that is now happening.

You have now moved into an inner mind power state of clear emotions. You are aware that your emotions change when your thoughts change.

In order for things to change you must change. You must first become aware of negative self-limiting beliefs... Once you are Aware... you can now change your thoughts to positive mind power beliefs that serve you. From this moment on, you will stretch your awareness to clear and positive thinking.

These suggestions are firmly embedded in your subconscious mind. They become stronger and stronger day by day... as you are now becoming aware of your thoughts. With this new awareness you are moving in a direction up the Emotional Energy Ladder™ through you own mind power thinking. You are aware.

Now - when you're ready - I'm going to count from one to five. When I reach the number five you'll be wide awake feeling fully rested, refreshed and energized.

Number one – Aware of the positive inner mind power now within you... as your body and mind have been relaxed, cleansed and revitalized.

*Number two – sensing a new **Awareness** of positive energy and emotions that has stretched in and around you.*

Number three – You are becoming aware of the material beneath you... Your breathing is becoming more regular, and you are coming slowly back to the place you started this journey.

Number four – feeling fantastic in every way... and on the next number you will be alert, recharged and refreshed with energy.

Number five – take a deep breath in, stretch your arms and open your eyes when you're ready

Welcome Back!

APPENDIX III - GRATITUDE

Affirmations:

Here are some affirmations on **Gratitude** based on what you've learned in that chapter.

Say these to yourself morning and night. Write them down and place them somewhere for daily viewing, like a bathroom mirror, refrigerator or nightstand. Read them often as repetition is the key to your development.

- I am Grateful for the gift to reach out and stretch my inner mind.
- I allow my thoughts of gratitude to enhance my golf and life.
- I am grateful for everything and everyone.
- Gratitude guides me to a higher level in my golf game.
- I am grateful to play golf at my personal best.
- I realize that faith is born of gratitude; I have complete faith in myself.
- I am so grateful for my life! Thank You, thank you, thank you.

Create your own Gratitude affirmations:

_____

_____

_____

Appendix

> *Find a quiet place where you won't be disturbed for 15-20 minutes. Turn off the phones and any disturbances. Recline or lie flat with your arms parallel to your body and feet separated. Make yourself comfortable. Read slowly taking an occasional pause between paragraphs.*

(Record the following or download it at www.yourinnerswing.com)

Begin by closing your eyes and taking a deep breath in, hold it for the mental count of three and exhale slowly, relax now. Take another deep breath in, and as you slowly exhale feel a wave of relaxation move from the top of your head all the way down your body to the tips of your toes, relaxing you even deeper.

Calmness and relaxation are beginning to flow down your body now - every nerve - every cell - every fibre - every consciousness of your body - is relaxing nicely now - relaxing - letting go of tension - letting go - let go.

And take just one more long, slow deep breath - hold it for three - and let go. Notice how heavy your hands are becoming now - so heavy - so comfortable and so relaxed. Let go.

And as you notice that heaviness there in your hands - feel it spreading all over your body - and let your eyes feel heavy as well - heavy and comfortable and so relaxed - let go of those muscles around your eyes - for it takes no effort whatsoever to allow them to remain comfortably closed.

Imagine little weights pulling down on your lashes - allowing your eyes to remain closed so that you can look up onto the screen of the forehead - and imagine the word - relax - relax - relax - or imagine a shape - or a color - or a sign - that can symbolize the word relax - and take that symbol of relaxation - back - and back - and back - until it relaxes both the left and the right lobes of the brain - and allow that relaxing feeling to flow all the way through your body - and let go.

As you drift deeper into this calm and comfortable feeling, you begin to feel a sense of gratitude for everything in your life right now. It's a wonderful feeling to really appreciate the natural state of being part of this beautiful Universe. This is your special time - your time to reflect on the wonders of life - your time to really feel grateful for all the seemingly little things that are a part of the whole and how important they really are in your life.

And you know that it's never too late to feel gratitude. You can really choose to be grateful for everything in your life right now - almost as though you were a small child again. Think back to the pure innocence of childhood - perhaps watching the snowflakes gently falling and settling on a windowpane or catching one on your tongue. Or maybe you'll remember watching springtime blossoms form from seeds, becoming flowers or plants or even trees that eventually grew big and strong - though you didn't realize at the time how those seeds would turn out.

Did you ever gather buttercups or search for four-leaf clovers along the road where you walked? Did you see the sun set and wonder where it would go? Or gaze at the stars on a velvety dark night and wonder at the life up there - in the galaxies far, far away? Were you fascinated by certain periods in history or geographical places? Did you have toys that you would play with for hours and hours, just mindlessly? Or did you ever see a new life being born?

We all have our own special memories of childhood days - they were a magical time - when anything was possible - where miracles could happen and our young minds soaked up everything like a brand new sponge in a tub of warm soapy water. Remember and appreciate your life through young eyes.

You can look through the eyes as a young child again... seeing each blade of grass - the perfection in a single raindrop or flower in full bloom maybe noticing the beautiful colors in nature or listen to the songs of the birds singing in the trees – feel the wind rustling through leaves, feeling so grateful for your sense of touch and smell and taste and so many other things you are now appreciating at a deeper level.

Unexpectedly the haze that's been clouding your vision begins to lift. All of your senses are sharpened - your mind is more focused and much more alert. Thoughts of gratitude give you such clarity in your heart... which is the highest and most wonderful emotion you can feel. It brings you unconditional love within you. You are now appreciating not only the good things in life - but everything, with the understanding of how it all falls together... eventually forming a perfect picture... like the pieces of a jigsaw puzzle.

When you watch people pass by - or observe them on a train or a bus - isn't it strange to think that you're not the central point in this world - all these people are experiencing their own inner world - just as you are - they're wrapped up in their thoughts and their lives.

You are grateful for your health - knowing that there are so many people out there in the world who are worse off than you - and what's more amazing is how they cope - and so often they do - adjusting to blindness, deafness, paralysis and other disabilities. You can feel compassion for these people as well as admiring how well they do - and this makes your gratitude for all things in life increase to an even greater height.

You find it easy now to express your gratitude to people in your life. You may even realize that a few little words can mean so much and simply giving thanks to someone in recognition of the effort they've put in to something can be like magic to their soul. People want to do more when they realize they're appreciated - most people want to please others and just be liked - for they are no different than you in this respect.

And appreciating all things in life makes you a happier and more agreeable person. Yes, there are times when things happen. You'll experience the lows as well as the highs - just like there's black and white, night and day, the sun and the moon - and this is good because without a few negatives - how would you recognize gratitude for feeling positive?

You find yourself becoming far more positive in all aspects of your life - you look on the bright side of life, seeing the good that will come out of any situation - and you become a happier and much more content person, a much more relaxed and more confident person in every way.

Now that you are becoming more and more conscious of gratitude day by day, the following affirmations will help you move in a more positive and appreciative direction. Repeat them in your mind:

- *I am Grateful for the gift to reach out and stretch my inner mind.*

- *I allow my thoughts of gratitude to enhance my golf and life.*

- *I am grateful for everything and everyone.*

- *Gratitude guides me to a higher level in my golf game.*

- *I am grateful to play golf at my personal best.*

- *I realize that faith is born of gratitude; I have complete faith in myself.*

- *I am so grateful for my life! Thank You, thank you, thank you.*

Insert your own affirmations or repeat the above.

_____

_____

_____

These suggestions are firmly embedded in your subconscious mind and grow stronger and stronger day by day... Stronger by the day, stronger by the hour - stronger by the minute.

Now in a moment - I'm going to count from one to five and at the count of five you'll be wide awake. The moment I reach the number five your body and mind will feel completely refreshed and revitalized, alert and awake.

Number one - sensing this feeling of gratitude has moved you up the emotional guidance ladder in body and mind.

Number two - feeling every muscle, nerve and fibre in your body has been showered with pure **Gratitude**.

Number three – You are becoming aware of the material beneath you... Your breathing is becoming more regular, and you are coming slowly back to the place you started this journey.

Number four – feeling fantastic in every way... and on the next number you will be alert, recharged and refreshed with energy.

Number five – take a deep breath in, stretch your arms and open your eyes when you're ready

Welcome Back!

APPENDIX IV - GOALS

Affirmations:

Here are some **Goal** affirmations that are based on what you learned in that chapter.

Say these to yourself morning and night. Write them down and place them somewhere for daily viewing, like a bathroom mirror, refrigerator or nightstand. Read them often as repetition is the key to your development.

- I create goals that help me stretch beyond my limitations.
- My goals help me improve my golf game in every way.
- I choose SMART goals that I write down and read daily.
- My goals drive me to improved thoughts, feelings and emotions.
- I love setting goals that improve my golf.
- I love to accomplish my goals and create more goals.
- I am a goal setter in golf and life.

Create your own Goal affirmations:

_____

_____

_____

> *Find a quiet place where you won't be disturbed for 15-20 minutes. Turn off the phones and any disturbances. Recline or lie flat with your arms parallel to your body and feet separated. Make yourself comfortable. Read slowly taking an occasional pause between paragraphs.*

(Record the following or download it at www.yourinnerswing.com)

Begin by closing your eyes and taking a deep breath in, hold it for the mental count of three and exhale slowly, relax now. Take another deep breath in, and as you slowly exhale feel a wave of relaxation move from the top of your head all the way down your body to the tips of your toes, relaxing you even deeper.

Calmness and relaxation is beginning to flow down your body now - every nerve - every cell - every fibre - every consciousness of your body - is relaxing nicely now - relaxing - letting go of tension - letting go - let go.

And take just one more long, slow deep breath - hold it for three - and let go. Notice how heavy your hands are becoming now - so heavy - so comfortable and so relaxed. Let go.

And as you notice that heaviness there in your hands - feel it spreading all over your body - and let your eyes feel heavy as well - heavy and comfortable and so relaxed - let go of those muscles around your eyes - for it takes no effort whatsoever to allow them to remain comfortably closed.

Imagine little weights pulling down on your lashes - allowing your eyes to remain closed so that you can look up onto the screen of the forehead - and imagine the word - relax - relax - relax - or imagine that you can see the word relax - or a shape - or a color - or a sign - that can symbolize the word relax - and take that symbol of relaxation - back - and back - and back - until it relaxes both the left and the right lobes of the brain - and allow that relaxing feeling to flow all the way through your body - and let go.

As you enjoy these wonderful feelings of calm and relaxation - your mind begins to open up to new possibilities in your life... which in the past you may have avoided for reasons of your own ... because you know that all too often people can deliberately sabotage their goals because some silly little thing at the back of their mind says, "no, I can't do this."

All this is changing for you now, because you deserve to be successful in whatever endeavour you choose. You work hard for your goal - and it's only natural that you should be rewarded in the way that is most important to you.

In a way it's like climbing a ladder and being afraid to take that very last step... the step to YOUR ULTIMATE Goal. You felt that something was holding you back. Now, you know that you have to move forward.

I wonder if you can imagine, now in your mind, a spiral staircase made out of stainless steel that seems to go up and around forever. It's an open staircase but you have your feet placed firmly upon each rung - and you begin to climb up. You can take any position that you want as you move up this staircase, because you trust in your subconscious mind, and you know it will not let you down.

And as you go farther and farther up this staircase, you may see people you love - either up, or halfway or even already at the top, it doesn't really matter where they are. The only important thing is that you know they are there for you, to see you thru and always will be.

You know that you have a goal to reach; sometimes you may even stop climbing and take a rest. A brief moment in hypnosis time can last just as long as you like, or you can keep on going, higher and higher.

There's something special awaiting you at the top of the staircase, you don't yet know what, and at the same time you do realize that it's worth it for you to keep climbing.

You have three choices. You can stay where you are, climb back down to the bottom, or you can keep on pursuing your goals, your dreams.

Which do you want to do?

You have already decided to rise up, and as you get higher and higher, you realize that nothing can hold you back, nothing can bring you down, because you're already well on your way. Yes, it may be scary at times, especially if you look down, not because you're afraid of heights, but because you realize that you've put in so much effort now and it wouldn't be fair to yourself to give up, so you keep on going.

And the higher you go, the easier it becomes. And the easier it becomes, the higher you go. There's no stopping you now - you're not far from where you want to go, from reaching your goal. Nothing in the world could make you stop now.

You go higher and higher, one step at a time, until suddenly - even though it seemed at the time to take so long to hit your target - you find that you're there. You're at the top of the staircase, and you still have your feet placed firmly on the rung of the step. You can hear people cheering you on. These are your inner inspirations and your internal motivations; they've been here with you all the time.

Now, you come to a plateau, an area of stability, and you have to leave this spiral staircase to explore all the new opportunities that are awaiting you. You ease yourself up, up from the staircase, looking around for a firm grip to hold onto, and there it is waiting for you. So you literally push yourself up from the last rung of the staircase and onto the new level that you've just reached. You've made it, you've done it! Doesn't it feel good?

Now, whatever your idea of success is, find it here, waiting for you. This is your time to explore it, enjoy it and experience it now. You worked hard to climb up and reach your goal, and you truly deserve to enjoy the rewards of your efforts.

Now that you are becoming more and more conscious of creating and achieving your goals... day by day... the following affirmations will help you move in a more positive direction. Repeat them in your mind:

- *I create goals that help me stretch beyond my limitations.*
- *My goals help me improve my golf game in every way.*
- *I choose SMART goals that I write down and read daily.*
- *My goals drive me to improved thoughts, feelings and emotions.*
- *I love setting goals that improve my golf.*
- *I love to accomplish my goals and create more goals.*
- *I am a goal setter in golf and life.*

Insert your own Goal affirmations (or repeat from above)

_____

_____

_____

Now you're doing what you really want to do. This is a gift for you, from you. You have been granted the inner mind power to achieve what you want, through your goals. Enjoy it now. Experience it now as I'm quiet while you take pleasure in this new feeling from within.

Good - and now that your mind has accepted that you can reach your goal, it will be so easy for you, because the neural pathways in your brain have been laid down, making it so much easier in the future to travel that path. You are a success, you deserve your success. Negative thoughts have been released as you realize they're not a part of your Baggage anymore. You know in order to achieve your goals you think positive, creative thoughts.

Enjoy this success and in a few moments, I'm going to count from one to five and at the count of five you'll be wide awake, feeling refreshed and alert and ready to begin your new adventure.

These suggestions are firmly embedded in your subconscious mind. They become stronger and stronger day by day... as you are now aware of the thoughts you need for creating and achieving goals. You are moving in the direction that creates your own mind power thinking for success on the golf course and in life.

When you're ready I'm going to count from one to five. When I reach the number five you'll be wide awake feeling fully rested, refreshed and energized.

Number one – feeling a new sense of energy in creating goals. Your body and mind have been relaxed, cleansed and revitalized.

Number two – you are now open to endless possibilities you create, through setting personal **Goals**.

Number three – You are becoming aware of the material beneath you... Your breathing is becoming more regular, and you are coming slowly back to the place you started this journey.

Number four – feeling fantastic in every way... and on the next number you will be alert, recharged and refreshed with energy.

Number five – take a deep breath in, stretch your arms and open your eyes when you're ready.

Welcome Back!

APPENDIX V - ATTITUDE

Affirmations:

Here are **Attitude** affirmations that are based on what you learned in that chapter.

Say these to yourself morning and night. Write them down and place them somewhere for daily viewing, like a bathroom mirror, refrigerator or nightstand. Read them often as repetition is the key to your development.

- My positive attitude empowers me on and off the golf course.
- I expand and stretch my attitude every day and in every way.
- I manage my golf game with a clear and optimistic attitude.
- My attitude helps me achieve all my goals.
- I am aware that my attitude makes me feel happy and joyful.
- My attitude attracts health, success and happiness from within.
- I inspire others with my bright and sunny attitude.

Create your own Attitude affirmations:

_____

_____

_____

Appendix

> *Find a quiet place where you won't be disturbed for 15-20 minutes. Turn off the phones and any disturbances. Recline or lie flat with your arms parallel to your body and feet separated. Make yourself comfortable. Read slowly taking an occasional pause between paragraphs.*

(Record the following or download it at www.yourinnerswing.com)

Begin by closing your eyes and taking a deep breath in, hold it for the mental count of three and exhale slowly, relax now. Take another deep breath in, and as you slowly exhale feel a wave of relaxation move from the top of your head all the way down your body to the tips of your toes, relaxing you even deeper.

In a moment I'm going to ask you to visualize certain things - and you'll find that by imagining the scenes I describe you will become so totally engrossed and absorbed that you will actually feel and experience yourself there.

I'd like you to create a magnificent day in your mind - you're out in the country - or some distant memory of a wonderful place that you've visited before. You're walking along a dirt road, with beautiful wild flowers growing on the side of the road. In the distance you can see a beautiful cottage - with a thatched roof - and it is surrounded by trees bearing white blossoms and pink and white roses which are in full bloom.

As a gentle breeze passes by, you may notice a sweet fragrance waft past your senses. Take a deep breath in now and fill you lungs with the pure clean air surrounding you. As you release the breath slowly you can relax to even deeper state. Feeling so relaxed, feeling so comfortable, feeling so easy.

Now imagine in your mind walking into this cottage and seeing a beautiful stairway with with colored lights. See the color green as an emerald, picture blue as a sapphire, vibrant red as ruby. There are just ten steps to reach the bottom. You are invited to go deeper down, down to a wonderful place - deep within yourself - and go down, down - deeper and deeper relaxed ...and let go.

Feel yourself moving down the stairs now. Step down to nine, and eight. See yourself going deeper down, seven - feel yourself going deeper down, six - but know that your mind is still here - listening to and hearing whatever is said, five, four - and very soon - as you go deeper - you'll achieve the perfect state of relaxation, three - letting go of distractions - for any noise - any sound - any movement you hear or sense - takes you deeper and deeper within yourself, two - so let go now... one.

You are now deeply relaxed and the suggestions that you hear will have a permanent and immediate effect on your subconscious mind - you will hear every word that I speak - even though you may find your mind wandering away at times - because right now - nothing else matters - nothing - except for this wonderful feeling of relaxation that you're experiencing.

At this moment it's as though you haven't a care in the world - nobody wants anything - nobody needs anything - there is absolutely nothing at all for you to do except relax and let go - and just enjoy the feelings that are being generated within you.

In this state of deep relaxation the critical factor of your conscious mind is also very deeply relaxed so that you can accept any suggestion or idea for your own good and well being. In this session while you are pleasantly relaxed you are going to be given words to think about. Just think lazily over these words. Let them sink deep into your subconscious mind.

The first word to picture in your mind is "health". Think of the word health as always coupled with the word "good". What can the words "good health" mean? They can mean a sense of optimum well-being, with a strong heart and lungs; perfect functioning of all the inner organs, nerves, muscles and systems of the entire body. It can mean strong bones and joints, an increased resistance to all forms of infection or disease, and greater control of the entire autonomic, hormonal and nervous system.

Good health not only means physical health. It means also a healthy attitude of mind. Imagine an attitude in which the nerves are stronger and steadier, the mind is crystal clear, more composed and tran-

quil and more relaxed and confident.

A healthy attitude can mean a greater feeling of self-esteem, a greater feeling of personal well-being, safety, security and happiness than has ever been felt before.

A healthy attitude can mean having complete control of your thoughts and emotions, with the ability to concentrate better and utilize all the vast resources of the memory and the full intellectual powers of the subconscious mind.

A healthy attitude can mean having the ability to sleep deeply and refreshingly at night and to awake in the morning feeling calm, relaxed, confident and cheerful - ready to meet all the challenges of the new day with boundless energy and enthusiasm. The words good health can mean to others any or all of these things and more. These words have tremendous power. Let them sink deeply into your subconscious mind, which can always reproduce in you your dominant thoughts.

The next word to think about is success. It may mean a sense of appreciation, a fulfillment or achievement of your desires. The success attitude opens all situations to all possibilities.

It may mean the ability to set and achieve goals in life that are realistic, worthwhile and progressive. The successful attitude opens the gates of motivation and determination to achieve those goals. It may mean the confidence of being able to throw off your inhibitions, being spontaneous, expressing your feelings without fear of hesitation.

Success may mean wealth in terms of money and the things that money can buy, or security for yourself and your family. It can also show itself in the attitude of mind which gives inner happiness regardless of material possessions or circumstances. It could mean the ability to overcome a particular challenge perhaps even some problem you may not be aware of. You can use the success attitude to walk taller, talk sweeter and produce better results. You choose the feelings which go with success.

The final word to think about is motivation. What is an attitude of motivation? It can mean a gradual and progressive strengthening of a desire to be in charge of one's life - o wipe out the old recordings of habits, remove Baggage, to play new music instead of old, to cease being pulled down by early programming and to become a creator of a new healthy happy successful script in the play of life.

The attitude of motivation can mean a gradual and progressive building of a stronger and stronger feeling of how positively others perceive you until your self-confidence is much stronger than your fear of failure. Achieving goals presents no difficulty, hardship or discomfort for you.

Repeat these Affirmations in your mind after hearing them

- *My positive attitude empowers me on and off the golf course.*
- *I expand and stretch my attitude every day and in every way.*
- *I manage my golf game with a clear and optimistic attitude.*
- *My attitude helps me achieve all my goals.*
- *I am aware that my attitude makes me feel happy and joyful.*
- *My attitude attracts health, success and happiness from within.*
- *I inspire others with my bright and sunny attitude.*

Create your own Attitude affirmations (or repeat from above)

_____

_____

_____

We have all been conditioned since birth to associate words with feelings. Words are therefore the tools which we are going to use to produce the feelings, attitudes and results which we want. And these words are health, success and motivation. The suggestions given to you are firmly embedded in your subconscious mind and grow stronger and stronger day by day... Stronger by the day, stronger by the hour - stronger by the minute.

In a moment I will slowly count from 1-5. When I reach the number five you will come out of the hypnotic trance you are now in. You will remember the suggestions given to you regarding health, success and motivation while hypnotized. You will incorporate these suggestions into your self-image. When you awake, you will feel deeply relaxed and you will remember being in hypnosis as an enjoyable and pleasant experience.

Number one - sensing this feeling of attitude has moved you up the emotional guidance ladder in body and mind.

*Number two - feeling every muscle, nerve and fibre in your body has been showered with pure positive **Attitude**.*

Number three – You are becoming aware of the material beneath you... Your breathing is becoming more regular, and you are coming slowly back to the place you started this journey.

Number four – feeling fantastic in every way... and on the next number you will be alert, recharged and refreshed with energy.

Number five – take a deep breath in, stretch your arms and open your eyes when you're ready.

Welcome Back!

APPENDIX VI - GARDEN

Affirmations:

Here are some affirmations for your **Garden** based on what you've learned in that chapter. Say these to yourself morning and night. Write them down and place them somewhere for daily viewing, like a bathroom mirror, refrigerator or nightstand. Read them often as repetition is the key to your development.

- I create new seeds of thought in my internal Garden every day.
- My Garden helps my golf game through new and beautiful growth.
- I control my inner Garden through positive thinking.
- My Garden is filled with beauty that enhances my love of golf.
- I choose to feed my Garden with new sprouting thoughts daily.
- My Garden is dynamic and abundant.
- I am my Garden and my Garden is me.

Find a quiet place where you won't be disturbed for 15-20 minutes. Turn off the phones and any disturbances. Recline or lie flat with your arms parallel to your body and feet separated. Make yourself comfortable. Read slowly taking an occasional pause between paragraphs.

(Record the following or download it at www.yourinnerswing.com)

Begin by closing your eyes and taking a deep breath in through your nose. Hold it for the count of three and exhale from your nose slowly. Relax now. Take another deep breath in, and as you slowly exhale, feel a wave of relaxation move from the top of your head all the way down your body to the tips of your toes, relaxing even deeper.

Calmness and relaxation is beginning to flow down your entire body now… from the top of your head - all the way down to the tips of the toes - every nerve - every cell - every fibre - every consciousness of your body - is relaxing nicely now - relaxing - letting go of tension - letting go - let go.

Now take another long, slow, deep breath - hold it for the count of three - and let the air release out of your nose, easily, slowly, going deeper and deeper.

Notice how heavy your hands are becoming now - so heavy - so comfortable and so relaxed. Let go. And as you notice that heaviness there in your hands - feel it spreading all the way over your body - and let your eyes feel heavy as well - heavy and comfortable and so relaxed - let go of those muscles around your eyes - for it takes no effort whatsoever to allow them to remain comfortably closed.

Imagine little weights pulling down on your lashes - allowing your eyes to remain closed so that you can look up onto the screen of the forehead - and imagine the word - relax - relax - relax - or imagine that you can see the word relax - or a shape - or a color - or a sign - that can symbolize the word relax - and take that symbol of relaxation - back - and back - and back - until it relaxes both the left and the right lobes of the brain - and allow that relaxing feeling to flow all the way through your body - and let go. Just let go where you will.

Now imagine you've found a beautiful magic carpet ... and you know that it's magic because of the wonderful colors on it. See the vibrant Green and purple and blue - and a magic gold star in the middle. Sit on the carpet and feel its texture – notice what it's made of. There are tassels on both ends of the carpet and they begin to sway and move as the carpet slowly lifts up, and up and up, into the air.

You're on the carpet and you can feel yourself being safely and comfortably lifted up as the carpet goes higher and higher.

Look around and see the trees and fields and houses... And as you go higher... feel yourself floating and relaxing even more. Maybe you can see the top of a church steeple and a small lake in the distance. And you are going over and past them - farther and farther away.

In the distance you can see a forest and you begin moving towards it. And from this height you can see everything below very clearly. As you're going over the forest now - and looking down you can see in the very middle of the forest - a beautiful white castle - with a drawbridge. Notice the shape of the doors and the windows. It looks so inviting that you decide to float down, and take a closer look at the castle.

And you're floating down now to the beautiful white castle below - going down - deeper - more relaxed - more comfortable - deeper and deeper relaxed.

And the further down you go the more relaxed and comfortable you become - and the more relaxed and comfortable you go - the deeper into this wonderful state of relaxation you travel. Going down now - deeper and deeper and deeper.

You've now reached the castle and landed your magic carpet. You're comfortably safe and very relaxed. There is a door in front of you. At the moment the door is closed - but very soon you're going to walk through that door - and when you do, you'll find yourself in a beautiful old country Garden.

When you're ready - I want you to gently push that door open - just push that door open - push with your mind - and the door opens easily for you - and you step through - closing the door and the ordinary everyday world behind you. Then look around and find yourself in the most beautiful Garden you've ever seen. You step out onto a stone patio with herbs and wildflowers and an old stone wall that partially surrounds the patio. Beyond the wall, on either side of you are beds of breathtaking fragrant flowers - opening their buds to the warmth of the afternoon sun. And you notice that sun shining on you now. It makes you feel so good inside. It makes you feel even more comfortable and more relaxed than every before.

As you hear the charming songs of various birds in the trees, you notice how some of those trees form an archway over a path which leads further into your magical Garden. You walk through the shaded archway and back into the sunshine - where there is a flower-filled wheelbarrow, a bird bath and a little-water filled stone for the birds to drink from. You look around taking in all the wonder and notice the beautiful delicate butterflies and buzzing bumble bees pollinating the tall fragrant flowers. All of your senses are engaged in this magical Garden, and you feel a sense of love all around you. Just in front of you are purple lilacs, fragrant lilies, orange sunset marigolds, feathery green ferns and ivy covered trees and trellises.

You feel so comfortable here - it's a beautiful magical place, full of peace and serenity. Each blade of grass looks unique to you - and you find yourself drifting deeper and deeper into calm, peacefulness and relaxation.

As you go deeper into the Garden you notice a sunken part of the Garden that you hadn't seen before. There are five little steps leading gently down - they were hidden before by the weeping willow and it looks so secluded down there - hidden away from the rest of the world - you hear the sound of trickling water even before you notice the water fountain - and a comfortable garden bench that is waiting for you. And you feel drawn towards this wonderful place.

So - go down those five steps now - one by one. Step down to the fourth step, easily and gently, three, relaxing deeper, down to two - feel yourself drifting deeper still - deeper and deeper and deeper relaxed. And now to the bottom step, one. So relaxed and calm.

Now walk over to the fountain and cup your hands - you're thirsty and the water here is clean and fresh - it comes from a natural underground spring and is the purest water you've ever tasted. Feel it trickling slowly between your fingers as you drink from this magical fountain, just a little is so refreshing and makes you feel good.

You're feeling quite sleepy now - so you rest on the bench nearby - and it's such a comfortable bench - that you close your eyes - still feeling the warmth of the sun on your face and the gentlest of breeze on your skin and your hair - and your eyes are closed as you lazily drift - into a beautiful peaceful dream.

And during this dream - your mind can wander - just as it will - you could go to the place you like best - or find a solution to all life's challenges - you can visit your creative self or reflect on a wonderful memory that you have - just go where you will - relax - and enjoy this time to yourself. (Pause for one minute)

Good - now bring your attention back to my voice. Whenever you wish to just let go and relax - or whenever you wish to find a solution to any problem you have - or to just visit your inner creative garden - you can do so easily - by closing your eyes and saying to yourself – Magical Garden - and the garden will spring to your mind - and you'll take yourself down the steps and into this wonderful place. And you'll be amazed at how good you feel when you return to normal conscious awareness - so refreshed and relaxed - yet alert and able to see clearly whatever you need to see or do.

Your subconscious mind is now open to suggestions for adopting a new garden. The following affirmations will help you move in a more positive direction. Repeat these in your mind after me:

- *I create new seeds of thought in my internal garden every day.*

- *My garden helps my golf game through new and beautiful growth.*

- *I control my inner garden through positive thinking.*

- *My garden is filled with beauty that enhances my love of golf.*

- *I choose to feed my garden with new sprouting thoughts daily.*

- *My garden is dynamic and abundant.*

- *I am my garden and my garden is me.*

Create your own Garden affirmations (or repeat the above)

_____

_____

_____

You know more than you think you know - you trust your subconscious mind, you love and respect yourself - you do good things for yourself - and you feel really good about yourself - this makes others feel good about you too.

In order to change anything in your life… you must first become aware of negative self-limiting beliefs… and change your thoughts into positive ones. From this moment on, you now choose clear and positive thoughts which add beautiful growth and energy to your inner garden.

These suggestions are firmly embedded in your subconscious mind… They become stronger and stronger day by day.

In a moment I'm going to count from one to five - at the count of five I want you to come back up those steps and return to normal conscious awareness - and bring back all those wonderful feelings with you feeling fully refreshed and energized. .

Number One – noticing you're filled with a positive mind power in your newly fertilized **Garden**... *as your body and mind have been relaxed, cleansed and revitalized.*

Number Two – sensing a new confidence, energy and love that have expanded in and around you.

Number Three – you are starting to notice the material beneath you… Your breathing is becoming more regular, and you are coming slowly back to the place you started.

Number Four – feeling fantastic in every way... and on the next number you will be alert, recharged and refreshed with energy.

Number Five – take a deep breath in, stretch your arms and open your eyes when you're ready.

Welcome Back!

APPENDIX VI - ENERGY

Affirmations:

Here are some **Energy** affirmations based on what you've learned in that chapter. Say these to yourself morning and night. Write them down and place them somewhere for daily viewing, like a bathroom mirror, refrigerator or nightstand. Read them often as repetition is the key to your development.

- I believe in the power to change my Energy whenever I wish.
- My Energy supports and enhances my golf game.
- I control my internal Energy through positive thoughts and deep breathing.
- My positive Energy supports my golf game in every way.
- I choose to feed my mind with healthy Energy.
- I attract dynamic and abundant life Energy all around me.
- I am Energy and Energy is me.

> *Find a quiet place where you won't be disturbed for 15-20 minutes. Turn off the phones and any disturbances. Recline or lie flat with your arms parallel to your body and feet separated. Make yourself comfortable. Read slowly taking an occasional pause between paragraphs.*

(Record the following or download it at www.yourinnerswing.com)

Begin by closing your eyes and taking a deep breath in, hold it for the mental count of three and exhale slowly, relax now. Take another deep breath in, and as you slowly exhale feel a wave of relaxation move from the top of your head all the way down your body to the tips of your toes, relaxing you even deeper.

And take just one more long, slow deep breath - hold it for three - and let go. Notice how heavy your hands are becoming now - so heavy- so comfortable and so relaxed. Let go.

And as you notice that heaviness there in your hands - feel it spreadingall over your body - and let your eyes feel heavy as well - heavy and comfortable and so relaxed - let go of those muscles around your eyes - for it takes no effort whatsoever to allow them to remain comfortably closed.

Imagine little weights pulling down on your lashes - allowing your eyes to remain closed so that you can look up onto the screen of the forehead - and imagine the word - relax - relax - relax - or imagine a shape - or a color - or a sign - that can symbolize the word relax - and take that symbol of relaxation - back - and back - and back - until it relaxes both the left and the right lobes of the brain - and allow that relaxing feeling to flow all the way through your body - and let go.

In a moment I'm going to ask you to visualize certain things - and you'll find that by imagining the scenes I describe you will become so totally engrossed and absorbed that you will actually feel and experience yourself there.

I'd like you to create a magnificent day in your mind - you're out in the country - or some distant memory of a wonderful place that you've visited before. You're walking along a dirt road, with beautiful wild flowers growing on the side of the road. In the distance you can see a beautiful cottage - with a thatched roof - and it is surrounded by trees bearing white blossoms and pink and white roses which are in full bloom.

As a gentle breeze passes by, you may notice a sweet fragrance waft past your senses. Take a deep breath in now and fill you lungs with the pure clean air surrounding you. As you release the breath slowly you can relax to even deeper state. Feeling so relaxed, feeling so comfortable, feeling so easy.

Now imagine in your mind a beautiful stairway with colored lights. See the color green as an emerald, picture blue as a sapphire, vibrant red as ruby. There are just ten steps to reach the bottom. You are invited to go deeper down, down to a wonderful place - deep within yourself - and go down, down - deeper and deeper relaxed ...and let go.

Feel yourself moving down the stairs now. Step down to nine, and eight. See yourself going deeper down, seven - feel yourself going deeper down, six - but know that your mind is still here - listening to and hearing whatever is said, five, four - and very soon - as you go deeper - you'll achieve the perfect state of relaxation, three - letting go of distractions - for any noise - any sound - any movement you hear or sense - takes you deeper and deeper within yourself, two - so let go now... one.

You are now deeply relaxed and the suggestions that you hear will have a permanent and immediate effect on your subconscious mind - you will hear every word that I speak - even though you may find your mind wandering away at times - because right now - nothing else matters - nothing - except for this wonderful feeling of relaxation that you're experiencing.

At this moment it's as though you haven't a care in the world - nobody wants anything - nobody needs anything - there is absolutely nothing at all for you to do except relax and let go - and just enjoy the feelings that are being generated within you. Repeat these affirmations in your mind after me:

- *I believe in the power to change my Energy whenever I wish.*

- *My Energy supports and enhances my golf game.*

- *I control my internal Energy through positive thoughts and deep breathing.*

- *My positive Energy supports my golf game in every way.*

- *I choose to feed my mind with healthy Energy.*

- *I attract a dynamic and abundant life Energy all around me.*

- *I am Energy and Energy is me.*

You know more than you think you know about your internal energy - you trust your subconscious mind, you love and respect yourself - you do good things for yourself - and you feel really good about yourself - this makes others feel good about you too.

In order to change anything in your life... you must first become aware of negative self-limiting beliefs... and change your thoughts into positive ones. From this moment on, you now choose clear and positive thoughts which add wonderful Energy to your inner being.

These suggestions are firmly embedded in your subconscious mind... They become stronger and stronger day by day.

In a moment I'm going to count from one to five - at the count of five I want you to come back up those steps and return to normal conscious awareness - and bring back all those wonderful feelings with you feeling fully refreshed and energized. .

Number One – noticing you're filled with a positive life-giving Energy... as your body and mind have been relaxed, cleansed and revitalized.

Number Two – sensing a new confidence, **Energy** *and love that have expanded in and around you.*

Number Three – starting to notice the material beneath you... Your breathing is becoming more regular, and you are coming slowly back to the place you started.

Number Four – feeling fantastic in every way... and on the next number you will be alert, recharged and refreshed with Energy.

Number Five – take a deep breath in, stretch your arms and open your eyes when you're ready.

Welcome Back!

ABOUT THE AUTHOR

Randy Friedman started playing racquetball at the age of nine, and competed professionally until she retired as the fourth-highest-ranked female player in the world. She then took up golf, and eventually began a full time career as an instructor, mind coach and speaker for golfers.

As a Golf Professional working at various country clubs, Randy has taught thousands of lessons to students of all ages on visualization and mind power. Today, she continues to entertain and educate audiences with corporate keynotes, golf workshops, and seminars. Her programs are notable for their passion, optimism, and practical advice.

As a speaker, mind coach, LPGA Teaching Professional, and author, Randy Friedman delivers *Your Inner Swing* as a keynote speech that inspires golfers — and everyone else — to breathe deep, focus on what they want and help them get out of their own way.

For information on professional speaking engagements, customized corporate golf, audio programs and other materials, please visit:

www.YourInnerSwing.com or www.GolfMindPower.com

Email: Randy@YourInnerSwing.com

Brandon Toropov - editor
www.iwordsmith.com

Anthony J. Parisi - illustrator & book design
www.parisistudios.com